Orange Peel Eclipse

stories

Eric Suhem

Contents

The following stories are presented with slight modifications from their previously published form.

Egg

Enid drove to the supermarket, relieved that the divorce papers had been finalized. Her now ex-husband Frank was probably in his usual location at this time of the day, shooting seagulls at the city dump. He was still calling her on the phone, asking her to take him back, and she was going to change the number.

Enid thought about her marriage on her way to the supermarket, and all that came into her mind was the night she told Frank that she was going to apply as a contestant on the game show Jeopardy. "Another one of your harebrained ideas, now why don't you do something useful and fix me some eggs," said Frank, plopping his butt onto a torn plastic chair at the kitchen table, expecting eggs scrambled, fried, hard-boiled, soft-boiled or poached, on his plate promptly at 6 p.m. every evening. Frank would continue crushing Enid's spirit with further commentary, as his incisors and molars tore at the eggs, the yolk dribbling down his chin.

But that was weeks ago, and now she was free. Arriving at the supermarket, Enid went to the poultry section and looked at the eggs. One of the eggs within a carton looked curious, and Enid felt drawn to it, so she pulled it out of the carton, put it in her shopping basket, and approached the checkout cashier. "I'd like to purchase this egg please," she said to the harried cashier, who looked quickly at the price chart near the register.

"Where is the carton with the rest of the eggs?" asked the cashier.

"There is no carton, I just want this one egg, please," Enid replied. The cashier was extremely vexed, and could already feel the clouds of impatience gathering among the other customers in line.

Eventually, Enid was able to purchase the egg and drove home, caressing it, shielding it from the elements. She arrived at her house, and placed the egg on a fuzzy fabric near the window, nestling it, keeping it warm and protected.

That night, Enid drifted into a dream....*she was inside a round white plastic container. It was pressing in on her shoulders, feet and head. The white container was being squeezed by forces from outside, forces of Frank, filled with fear. Enid felt the power of her imagination, the surface of the white container expanding, and then exploding! She staggered from the pale orb, emerging into a strange dark meadow. Hens were staring at her from behind the weeds. Enid moved around in the meadow, listening to the hens recite Jeopardy game show questions. "I'll take 'Autonomy' for 800, Alex," Enid murmured as the hens ran about busily. She saw a bright red phone booth across the field. Its phone was ringing. "Your destiny's calling, are you accepting the charges?" asked one of the hens dramatically.*

Enid awoke from the dream, just as a bird was hatching from the egg. The bird had Enid's face. She looked at the chick and could feel relief and empowerment start to grow within. The phone rang, and she knew it was that creep, her ex-husband Frank, so she just let it ring. For some reason, she still hadn't changed the number. Enid then looked at the face of the bird, which slowly morphed into Frank's angry countenance. It glared up at her as the phone continued to ring. She thought briefly about giving Frank another chance, taking him back again, but no, she would not answer the phone this time. Instead, she put the cracked egg containing the Frank-bird into a plastic bag and drove to the supermarket to get a refund, but the supermarket was gone.

(originally published in **Winamop**)

In Defense of Bowling

'Further Adventures from the Casebook of Dottie Nettles, Bowling Shop Proprietress'

Monday, June 13, 1958, was like any other day as I maneuvered my avocado-colored sedan into the bowling center parking lot. There were plenty of open spaces in which to park, but I wasn't satisfied with any of them. "I need strategic positioning," I murmured, as my huge Chrysler circled the lot.

Suddenly the news on the car radio was interrupted by a special bulletin: "Attention all bowlers, it has been reported that there is a conspiracy by Communist organizations to alter the lane conditions at all bowling centers in order to guarantee higher scores and more pin action for leftist bowlers (I imagined left-handed bowlers) If you are witness to any inappropriate alterations of lane conditions, contact your nearest American Bowling Association office, and we'll send out a combat force!"

"I thought to myself, "Hmm…interesting, but how is this going to concern **me**?"

I entered the bowling center and bought a pack of wintergreen gum from the vending machine. I was met by a line of people, each demanding something. A quivering shadow of a man approached with his bowling ball. "Dottie, Dottie! I need to have this thumbhole sanded for tonight's tournament! Can you do it in time?"

"Not a problem," I calmly replied.

"I…I need it sanded and nobody else in town can do it." He trembled like a bowl of tangerine-flavored jello.

"**Sit down**!" I ordered. It was then that I saw them, skulking past the 'Bowler's Accessories' machines. They were the subversive bowlers, preparing for team league play, and an attack on our American way of life. Instead of using their real name, 'Workers Struggling for Better Bowling,' they were calling themselves the 'Alley Cats'. I knew they were smuggling nonstandard red bowling balls into the alley, which guaranteed greater pin action and higher scores.

"Dottie, Dottie…are you all right? Wh-what about my thumbhole?" the quivering man was asking, but I didn't hear him, I was deep in thought.

"This subversive activity is making me…**mad!**" I whispered, fist clenching.

"They're not a threat, are they?" asked my assistant, arranging bowling shoes on a shelf.

I had faced up to threats since I was 4 years old when a lump of shirts on the back of the chair in the middle of the night formed a menacing presence. I defeated that threat, and I would defeat this one too. "There's always a threat," I replied, spitting the wintergreen gum out into a plastic ashtray.

I then realized that the gum had been drugged by the subversive bowlers with a substance concocted in a remote Siberian gulag. I slipped into hallucinations, staring at the pinball machines in the bowling center…*The pilgrims danced around the nectarine pinball machine, calling out the names of all the poultry quality-control inspectors that they knew, thus they were silent. The silver ball bounced around in the nectarine pinball machine as red-suited insurance salesmen congregated ominously….*

I was shaken from this reverie by the leader of the subversive bowlers, who had taken the bowling shoe off of his left foot (size 8.5) and slammed it on an alley-side table, yelling "We will bury you!" He then put his shoe back on and returned to league play.

The subversive bowlers won all 3 of their games, by very questionable means in my opinion. As league activity completed, they packed up their red bowling balls and exited the alley. They got into their Volga compact car and attempted to leave the parking lot, but were obstructed by my huge Chrysler, parked in front of their exit path. "I knew I had a good reason for parking it there," I said, leisurely walking into the darkness of the parking lot, swinging my bowling ball bag to and fro, soon to implement my own version of mutually assured destruction.

The Sunshine Ghosts

The children disembarked the bus on a cold autumn day, carrying permission slips on a field trip to the aquarium. As they marched along, they could feel the energy rising up in steam from the ground. Nearby was the site of a sunshine be-in festival from long ago. Some of the children veered away from the field trip and headed toward the festival site, soaking up vibrations, happy little tie-dyed organic molecules gliding into their pores. At the end of the day, all of the children got back onto the bus. One of the children, Juliana, found some seeds on the ground under an apple tree and put them away in her lunch box. Along with the seeds was a piece of paper, upon which were written the words, 'Find the medicine man in the windmill forests'.

Years later, throughout her professional life, Juliana had not fit in. She worked as an office administrator, but her soul was not in tune with it. "Juliana, I need this memo processed immediately," said her manager in the lunch room, but Juliana was staring at the coffee pot, seeing fluorescent apples cascading down a hill towards an office park. In her vision, the avalanche of Gravensteins exploded onto the corporate landscape, through the open door of an office building, crashing against the light brown imitation wood-grain cabinets in the cafeteria, rattling the green Formica countertops, where the twisting tendrils crawl along the ancient Mayan mask. "Juliana, straighten up, or this will be a matter for Human Resources," said her manager. Juliana recognized the vision of tumbling apples as a dream she'd had the previous night.

After work that day, while looking through her closet, she discovered her lunch box from the childhood field trip of long ago, still containing the seeds and the instructions to search for the medicine man. Grabbing the seeds, Juliana hopped into her Toyota Camry, and sped onto the Great Highway, along the waves of the ocean, past the cliffs and sand dunes populated by the sunshine ghosts, heading east toward the windmill forests.

She drove all night until reaching the woods, the rattling

Toyota Camry knowing instinctively where to find the medicine man's rustic cabin. He was busy supervising the shampooing of his carpets but managed to give Juliana instructions on how to dispatch the seeds. Soon she was back in the car, leaving the forest, and approaching the dry brown hills where the massive windmills stood. Under the hot sunlight, Juliana trudged up the dirt road in her rubber-soled sandals, and buried the seeds exactly 9 feet due west of the third windmill, per the medicine man's instructions.

After planting the last seed, Juliana walked back down the dirt road. Hearing a rumbling, she looked up the hill, seeing green apples slowly tumbling down towards her. As the apples passed by, she picked one up. Juliana saw her 7-year old face on the apple peel, looking back at her. In fact, all of the apples had her face, as it looked when she had been on that field trip to the aquarium years ago. A hazy figure in an ancient Mayan mask appeared. Juliana recognized the figure as one of the sunshine ghosts, and said, while staring at the face on the apple peel, "I've lost this person, can you help me find her?"

"Let me show you," said the sunshine ghost, oozing with maternal bliss.

Within weeks, large beautiful tie-dyed flowers and apple trees were growing by the windmills, where the seeds had been planted. Juliana stopped working in administrative office jobs and went back to school to get a teaching credential. Soon she was teaching 2nd graders, arranging field trips to the aquarium and other haunts of the sunshine ghosts.

(originally published in *The Odd*)

Detour

I was in my car on the freeway, stuck in traffic. Staring at the jackhammers, steamrollers, and drying cement of the nearby paving project, I thought about the dreams that had transformed my world into a dark labyrinth from which there was no escape. In every dream, there was Thelma, wearing black, at the wheel of her dark coupe, headlights speeding toward me, the nightmare always ending with the crash of jagged metal.

The scorpions were crawling over the roadmaps in my Chevy sedan when the cell phone rang. It was Thelma, whose voice I hadn't heard in years, except in my dreams. "It's my husband…he's vanished…he fell down a manhole and nobody can find him in the sewers… I didn't know where else to turn…" I was about to hang up when I realized that dealing with Thelma head-on might be the only way to end the shattering nocturnal visions. We agreed to meet at her favorite cafe, a grimy pit named The Empty Spoon.

At the cafe, she looked the same as I'd remembered, though with a few more miles on the odometer. "I never thought I'd see you again," Thelma murmured, referring obliquely to our troubled past as co-workers in the city's sewer department. As we talked, I stared into her eyes, seeing nothing but black obsidian, and traffic hazards. Against my better judgment, I agreed to help her. She gave me the location of the manhole and then drove off, her black coupe careening down the road and veering toward pedestrians, the street's seediness igniting a gleam in her eyes.

Thinking about our past in the sewers, I arrived at the manhole in question and found the lid tightly shut. I tried to pry it open, when a street sweeper turned a corner and headed toward me, its headlights shining. I dived onto the sidewalk, evading the sweeper's brushes by inches. As the cleaning vehicle turned around, I dashed to my car, got in, and sped off.

Following a detour sign down a side street, I noticed a number of orange-vested workers fill the road, holding up 'Stop' and 'Slow' signs to each other as they moved around on the pavement, surrounding my car. More of them appeared, quickly covering the entire block, bumping into each other, waving flags, and hitting my car with orange plastic red cones. When they attacked my car with the 'Slow' signs, I decided I could wait no longer, and slowly plowed my car through the threatening sea of orange, flipping them onto the hood of my car, their leering grins pressed up against the windshield.

The mysterious street sweeper lurked nearby as I turned a corner and suddenly saw Thelma standing in the street in her black pantsuit. I stopped the car and got out, walking toward her, then halting when I saw the business end of the .38. "You had to pass me up for that promotion at the sewer department years ago, well you've reached a dead end," she said, pointing the gun.

"Now I know why you always wear black, because the colors tremble and fall off of you," I said in a measured tone, eyeing the oncoming street sweeper over Thelma's shoulder. As she cocked the trigger, the omnipresent cleaning vehicle was suddenly upon her, pulling her into its efficient maw and brushes as it moved along the dark pavement and disappeared around the corner.

I got back into my Chevy sedan and took a deep breath. It had been a day of desolation, doom, hazards, and orange vests. Thelma was gone, but she would be back in my dreams that night, and the next....

(originally published in *Weirdyear*)

Something in the Water

"Howard, get me some water!" ordered Manager #5 to one of his subordinates, as the management team of Acme MegaCorp gathered in the conference room to explore ideas designed to improve employee productivity and morale. "I suggest we add a mood-enhancing substance to the company's drinking water. A number of drugs have been very effective in experiments on dogs, cats and pigs," said Manager #5, staring moodily into his coffee mug. The management team approved the proposal for altered tap water.

Two days later, Howard was called into his manager's office. "Howard, we'd like you to be the point man for a new company-wide high-profile project. In fact, you'll be our guinea pig," said Manager #5, handing him a plastic cup of enhanced water. "Now drink this, and give me a report later."

"Yes, sir!" said Howard, grateful to be chosen for an important project. He'd always been a good team player. Maybe now it would pay off.

Back at his desk, arranging memos and paper clips into a geometric order that felt pleasing, Howard had a vision of a large guinea pig, sitting in the chair across from him, pounding its paw on the desk, **"Let's close the deal now, H.B.! And I won't take 'No' for an answer!"** The guinea pig threw its head back and laughed, pulling a scythe out from under the table.

Wielding the scythe given to him by the guinea pig, Howard went to the lobby and sliced up various artificial plants and topiary efforts, hacking rhythmically as a secretary looked on in horror. Later that day, Manager #5 called him into his office. "Howard, we need to discuss your behavior, upper management has taken an interest in your cutting of the welcoming area's greenery," said Manager #5, starting right in on an assessment of Howard's workplace conduct, using the word 'failure' 12 times, Howard's smile brightening each time he heard the word.

"I think it's great!" said Howard, in a good mood after drinking the enhanced water.

"Look, Howard, we're going to install a training wheel in your cubicle. "It will help you work off that energy in less destructive ways. You know, like a hamster or a guinea pig," said Manager #5.

As the days went by, the drugged water increased Howard's productivity and morale, which pleased the management team. Howard exercised vigorously on his little wheel, and some of the secretaries walked by his cubicle to feed him shredded lettuce.

One morning in his cubicle, Howard found the large guinea pig sitting at the desk. "Howard, we have to talk," whispered the guinea pig, beckoning Howard to have a seat on the training wheel. "Howard, you don't like this job, do you? It's demeaning and humiliating. You've played by the rules for your entire career, and look where it's gotten you."

Sitting on the training wheel, chewing shredded lettuce from his little bowl that was adorned with pictures of rodents at play, Howard felt something open up in his imagination. He'd always felt trapped in his job, and he hadn't been able to visualize himself doing anything else. But staring at the guinea pig, ideas began to flow: maybe he could join an organization that cares for and protects guinea pigs….maybe he could start a business building guinea pig cages…maybe become a chef that cooks guinea pigs in Cusco, Peru, near Machu Picchu. He wasn't sure if it was due to the water, but for the first time, he felt free, aware of options he hadn't realized.

Howard went to his manager's office to resign, bringing the scythe with him.

(originally published in *Linguistic Erosion*)

Blue Glow #7

He never felt more purposeful, being used as a polo mallet in the game of the gods, whacking a blue ball over the horizon glow.

(originally published in *Nailpolish Stories – a literary journal with stories of exactly 25 words*)

From the Eye

Amelia worked the counter at the health food emporium, with flowers in her hair and a beatific smile, butterflies flying in a gentle rhythm around her head. In the back of the emporium, her co-worker Violet sorted and stacked organic inventory.

"Good morning, isn't it a beautiful day?" cooed Amelia to the next customer, a man in a dark suit and sunglasses approaching the counter clutching a bottle of multivitamins. He didn't reply, just spilled a bag of coins on the counter, meticulously separating them into distinct piles. Amelia felt a slight flare of annoyance, waiting for him to finish. When done, he flipped off his sunglasses, declaring, "I do believe this completes our transaction." The man's left eye resembled a gleaming green flower, and it cut into Amelia's soul like a floral laser, promising transcendence.

For the next seven nights, Amelia's dreams were dominated by the green flower. When waking up, her mind was filled with chlorophyll blossoms. Amelia told Violet, "We need to find the green flower. I believe it will lead us to a mystical answer!"

"Well, there's a plant nursery up the street, with lots of flowers, shrubs, and…."

"No, this was a special flower, a flower leading through the gates of nirvana into a gentle meadow of wonder and peace. An emergence from turbulent pain of the past into a shining future," said Amelia, butterflies fluttering nearby.

Amelia has a little man dancing around inside of her. The man has green flowers growing out of his eyes. When Amelia is happy, the little man is tickling her with the flowers, rolling about on Amelia's insides joyously…when Amelia feels low, the little man steps in, objectifying the pain, molding it like a mound of acid clay into a useful urn. Sometimes he's able to mold chunks of it, sometimes the clay just slips through his fingers. But slowly, ever so slowly, he is molding it. This is when the little green flowers in his eyes truly grow.

Walking home after a day of work at the health food emporium, Amelia stared at a bucolic garden of flowers. Turning a corner, she saw the man she'd encountered at the health food emporium. "It's you!" Amelia declared as the man peered out from behind sunglasses. "The flower in your eye imprinted itself upon my soul," she said.

The man looked at her, and pulled off his sunglasses, revealing clear green eyes, not flower-like at all. "Yes, my defective contact lenses reflected streaks of light haphazardly in shapes that could be perceived as flowers. However, I did enjoy the multivitamins I purchased at your establishment, as I believe they have contributed to an enhanced sense of well-being. Now if you'll excuse me, I'd like to proceed down this sidewalk unimpeded." Amelia stared at him, noticing his resemblance to her ex-husband. She thought of past promises destroyed, her parents self-destructing in an inferno of dysfunction, her ex-husband lashing out in abuse after seeming so kind. Amelia had meticulously built a wall of new age self-preservation, depending on a tenuous combination of chimes and mantras while searching for a transforming answer.

When Amelia gets angry, she wishes to send the little man within her out into the world with a molten hot hammer, killing and destroying the objects of her anger. But then a lasso is tied around the little man, and he spins around inside of Amelia, flower petals flying out of his tiny eyes to be pinched between the two fingers of Amelia's social conscience.

Enraged that mystical transcendence would again not be attained, Amelia decided to let the little man out into the world with his molten hot hammer, the flowers from his eyes turning black.

(originally published in ***Winamop***)

19

Mel and Alma

Alma sat at the rickety kitchen table, wearing a faded pink bathrobe, flicking ashes from her cigarette into a cup of cold coffee, a crack running through a scenic mountain panorama on the cup. The clock said 5:38 a.m. and the crossword was half done as she stared at the tattered curtains. In a couple of hours, she and Mel would go to the coffee shop, as they did every morning. The coffee shop had a large broken coffee cup sign on its roof. In the torn plastic booths, she and Mel would make their breakfast orders: a poached egg, coffee, and toast for Alma; pancakes, bacon and coffee for Mel.

Alma and Mel lived in a 2nd-floor apartment of the Palm Vista Village on a slightly seedy, wilted-palm tree street in Los Angeles. Alma griped about the neighborhood, but Mel would just smile, saying "One day we'll go on that vacation you want!" before heading off to work at one of the El Segundo aircraft factories. Only four more years to retirement.

On a hot, sweltering Tuesday morning, Mel had a hunch. He entered the bank as soon as it opened, requesting a withdrawal of the couple's life's savings. After a considerable delay of paperwork, Mel left the bank with the money. He arrived at their apartment, where Alma was vacuuming the worn, faded carpeting while watching television. "C'mon honey, we're going to the track!" yelled Mel, changing into his lucky Hawaiian shirt. Alma looked up from her vacuum, annoyed. "I got a hunch," said Mel, giving her that light wink of the eye that she loved. He showed her the travel pamphlet he'd been reading.

They got into their battered Toyota Camry and drove out to Hollywood Park. Alma looked askance at the burlap bag Mel clutched as they walked to the ticket window. "Number 7 to win in the 5th race," said Mel, pouring all of their money out of the burlap bag onto the scratched steel counter. The man at the window squinted briefly and gave Mel his ticket.

Mel and Alma both awoke on the ice floe, the ship nowhere in sight. The last either of them remembered was lounging on the main deck, each drinking a 'yellow canary', the specialty of the ship's bar. The horse they had bet on days ago, Number 7 in the 5th race, had won, and they'd collected the winnings quickly. They'd celebrated with a couple of chili dogs at a food stand, Mel staining his Hawaiian shirt. Mel and Alma had followed the directions on the vacation pamphlet, and boarded the majestic boat in San Pedro, ready for the "vacation of a lifetime". Mel thought he remembered a couple of dark figures approaching him on the deck and holding a chloroform-soaked cloth to his face, but he wasn't sure.

As the large chunk of ice approached land, Alma and Mel saw dozens of television screens, some affixed to the sides of buildings, some lodged in hillsides, some floating in the water near the shore. All of the television screens displayed large eyeballs staring back at Mel and Alma. A man in a dark sweater and goggles was digging in the sand when he saw the ice approaching. He threw up his hands and yelled "Hallelujah!" running toward Mel and Alma as the floe slid onto the sand. "Our leaders have arrived!"

"Where are we?" asked Alma, dazed and staring at an eyeball on the television screen at the end of the beach. As Mel and Alma looked further at the hills beyond the beach, they saw more television screens planted in the dirt, each screen displaying an eyeball. Mel bit his lip, thinking about the vacation they could have had, described in that other pamphlet. Alma stared into the eyeball, entranced.

(originally published in *Linguistic Erosion*)

My Digital Reality

Day 1

I love gadgets. That is, anything high-tech, cutting-edge. I keep up on all the latest developments in Silicon Valley. My blog is state-of-the-art, monitoring the newest innovations on the technological frontier. Needless to say, I am plugged in 24x7!

I work at a company called DigiGrab, and we are one of the leaders in the field. I am testing a new digital camera, as part of a beta program for one of our vendors. I take pictures with this new camera, and the cool thing is, whatever I take a picture of disappears, replaced only by the digital photo in my camera! If I delete that photo, it's like the subject never existed!

Day 2

I took the digital camera to the art museum. Unfortunately, there were some other people in the gallery. It seems that they wanted to just look at the art, to linger over it. They were in my way, preventing me from getting a clear shot. Eventually, I managed to weave my way through, and I got some direct lines at the paintings. Indeed, as soon as I clicked the shutter button, the paintings disappeared, remaining only in my camera. I was excited about the beta program results we'd be reporting to the upper-level management at DigiGrab!

I had been patient, but the people continued to get in my way. I had told myself I wouldn't do this, but couldn't resist taking the picture of a particularly loud, obstructive man. As with the paintings, he quickly disappeared. I took pictures of others: that languorous woman in a hat, the hyperactive child with a popsicle, the badgering senior citizen in a wheelchair, the lemur that had wandered into the museum and was clawing at my leg. They all vanished, reappearing only in the view screen of my digital camera. I reviewed their images, and, finding them disagreeable, deleted them to my camera's trash bin.

I left the museum and walked down the street, taking pictures of some of the exciting new gadgets and electronics in the store windows. When I got home, I snapped a shot of my fruit bowl, which soon disappeared into the camera. My curiosity got the best of me, and I had my wife take a picture of me in front of my house. The camera executed flawlessly, causing me and my house to disappear, replaced only by a digital photo and an empty dirt lot, where the house used to be. I sent a text message to my wife's smartphone: "I'm now surrounded by the subjects of my digital photos: great paintings, the people from the museum who had annoyed me at first, but now have become good friends, the lemur chewing on my leg, the electronic gadgets, the pears from my fruit bowl. I like it better here in the digital universe." And indeed I do.

Day 3
Inevitably, the batteries of the digital camera started to run down. My wife elected not to recharge them. She viewed my image one more time on the camera view screen, but the power flickered, and I slow..ly....wen...t........a....wa...y............

Day 4
Now I'm in the middle of nothing. Not even a cold, dark speck of dust. Just desolation, a void, an extinguishing spark of zero. Blankness rises from the east, disintegration appears from the west. The winds blow emptiness right and left. I set up a little stand in the midst of nothingness. The stand has nothing to offer, nothing to sell. It is desolate, in the middle of null. A cloud drifts up to my stand, and I ask if it has any batteries.

"No, but I like your minimalist aesthetic," says the cloud, before vanishing back into the nothingness.

I stare out into the barren emptiness and feel pleased. This is the way I like it. Nothing has happened yet. It's all new, free and clear, except for the lemur chewing on my leg, it is always there. My identity is a blank slate that I can redefine. I await a new technology.

(originally published in ***Hobo Pancakes***)

Tooth Art

Beverly had always wanted to be an artist of some sort, perhaps a painter or dancer, indenting brilliance upon the culture. She pictured herself in the New York art scene, wearing black, a fixture at galleries and performance spaces, reveling in the idea of high art.

Instead she was known as the 'Teen Dream Beauty Queen' of the snow-covered prairie, competing in beauty pageants since she was 5 years old. Over the past years, she had done well in the pageants, thanks to her award-winning teeth. Beverly's teeth were simply superb, and they compensated for any other blemishes and imperfections during the fine-toothed rigors of beauty pageant judging. Often her teeth shone a shimmering dagger of white light that temporarily blinded the audience, some viewers opting for special industrial-strength sunglasses. Based on Beverly's tooth prowess alone, her mother wanted the beauty pageant career to extend indefinitely, as the teeth had garnered adoration and tiaras.

"I want to be a ballet dancer that touches people's lives with an expression of my soul," said Beverly, "Or a painter, pouring my emotions out onto the canvas."

"But your teeth touch people's lives, look at these letters," said her mother, showing Beverly the scrapbook of testimonials by those whose lives had been transformed by viewing Beverly's oral enamel. In response to this, Beverly frowned, not displaying her riveting teeth at all.

"All right," said Beverly's mother, "I'll sign you up for a painting class."

Soon Beverly was enrolled in an Abstract Expressionism class, and enjoyed it, though her instructor wanted her paintings to include abstract molars, incisors, and canines, as this seemed to be what she painted best. "The teeth are the art that rings true for you," said her instructor.

Beverly was vexed by the emphasis on her teeth, both in the pageants and her paintings. One evening, after a demanding session with her Tooth Coach, Beverly went home and fell asleep early, drifting into a dream:

> *She was in a field of bright yellow flowers. She picked one of the flowers and held it to her mouth. Nectar tasting like a tonic from the gods oozed onto her tongue. Suddenly a dental chair appeared in the field, and the scene transformed into a dental office. The dentist was a parent of one of Beverly's beauty contest competitors. Under bright pageant lights, as his daughter practiced her baton twirling amidst the dental drills and spit sink, the dentist removed all of Beverly's teeth. Though now unnecessary, he placed a complimentary toothbrush, a tube of toothpaste, and dental floss in Beverly's hand.*

When Beverly woke up from the dream, she discovered that all of her teeth were gone, though she did find a toothbrush, toothpaste, and dental floss in her hand. She looked in the mirror and smiled, sensing possibilities.

"Beverly, what happened to your teeth!?" screamed her mother, looking up in shock from the beauty pageant schedule, and then fainting. Beverly wrote a long note to her mother and packed a suitcase. She walked to the bus station and bought a one-way ticket to New York City. On the bus seat, she found a dog-eared paperback copy of Freud's 'The Interpretation of Dreams', describing his theory of dreams as wish fulfillment.

In Manhattan, using some of the beauty pageant cash winnings she'd earned, Beverly bought a set of dentures, though she wore them infrequently, preferring instead to go toothless, making gumming noises. In avant-garde New York City clubs, Beverly started a career as an experimental performance artist, holding a microphone up to her rubbing gums, creating a new kind of music, becoming the artist she knew she'd be.

(originally published in *Smashed Cat*)

The Eggplant

On the flight, the stewardess moved down the aisle with a cart of refreshments. She eyed the passenger in seat 17A warily, as it was an eggplant. The eggplant was securely fastened with a seatbelt. "Why did you put an eggplant in seat 17A?" the stewardess asked the passenger in seat 17B.

"I have no idea why this eggplant is here, can you move me to another seat?" the passenger asked the stewardess, feeling uncomfortable as the eggplant nuzzled its purple skin against the blue synthetic fabric of the airplane seat.

"I'm sorry, but the flight is full," said the stewardess, who was soon on the phone to the flight reservations desk, asking about the name of the passenger in seat 17A. "It just says 'Eggplant'," said the reservations person, looking at a computer screen. "But the seat is paid for."

Accepting the situation, the stewardess asked the eggplant what it would like from the refreshment cart. The eggplant made no response or movement when the stewardess offered coffee or tea. When the stewardess asked the eggplant if it would like to be sprayed with a water bottle, it bounced up and down within the confines of the seatbelt, so she gave it a few spritzes.

As the flight progressed, the passenger in 17B decided that the eggplant was a good listener, and proceeded to regale it with a full account of the events that had led to her divorce, replete with an extensive description of her ex-husband's infidelities. The eggplant fulfilled a role as a competent sounding board.

A man walked by and told the eggplant that it reminded him of some of his finest dining experiences around the globe. "In France, I had a marvelous ratatouille with eggplant and zucchini in a Paris café by the Seine. In India, I enjoyed a sumptuous eggplant curry at a beautiful sun-filled restaurant. In Italy, an eggplant was prominent in my transcendent parmigiana di melanzane near the golden hills of Tuscany."

The woman in seat 17B grew impatient listening to the man go on and on about his travel adventures, feeling that the man was dominating the eggplant's listening time. She had more to say about her divorce, leaning over to whisper to the eggplant, "I'd like to talk with you some more about this when you get a chance."

At the conclusion of the flight, the woman in 17B and the global trekker both asked the eggplant whether it had a connecting flight. The eggplant remained noncommittal. When the man reached into seat 17A to grab the eggplant, the woman in 17B hit him with an inflight magazine. As the flight crew stepped in to lead the man and woman off the plane, the eggplant rolled down the aisle and out the exit as well, but not before the stewardess cut off a large chunk of its purple fruit, to be inserted into lunch sandwiches for the next flight. During meal service, she would say that the sandwiches were in honor of one of her favorite passengers.

(originally published in *Sensors C. Diff*)

The Joy of Gray

Alan worked on invoices in a small gray cubicle in Building #3 at Acme MegaCorp, Inc. On his desk were a stapler, tape dispenser, computer monitor, keyboard, mouse, papers, paperclips, inbox, outbox, and Kleenex box. Alan found the environment and the items on his desk exciting and stimulating, burrowing down to the core of his essence, igniting his soul into a flaming inferno. As the other employees trudged into work and slumped down at their desks, Alan would arrive, get his cup of coffee, sit upright in his cubicle, and be nearly brought to orgasm by the vision of the stapler at the corner of his desk.

Alan walked into the office break area. Just looking at his shoes easing into the gray fiber carpeting caused so much joyful electricity to shoot through his spine and brain that Alan had to return to his desk, sweating from overstimulation. He looked at the new Kleenex box on the left corner of his desk. This new box had gray swirly designs on it, instead of the previous box's blue swirly designs. Upon viewing this, Alan could not contain the hard pressure valve on the vivid roses, tape, glue, irises, effluvium, medicated leaves, staples, and replica paper ponies flowing out of his head, and he ran through the office area, screaming exuberantly.

Alan's employers at Acme MegaCorp, Inc. decided that he needed a vacation, arranging a mandatory trip for him to a beautiful tropical island. When Alan got off the plane, he looked at the brilliant green trees, blue sky, and white sand. He felt a grey tiredness taking over, and it increased with each bright color viewed, causing his eyelids to slowly close, until an accidental entrance into the resort's utility room, with its gray machinery, pipes, and walls revived him, and he ended up enjoying his vacation, though most of it was spent in the gray utility room.

It wasn't always this way. Alan used to love color, in fact, more so than most people. He remembered when he would commute to the office and look at the billboards, thinking, "What if all of these billboards were brilliantly hued designs, if there

were bright, colorful murals everywhere, instead of grayness?"
Back then, Alan had vivid posters in his cubicle and colorful
work tools on his desk. That was when Acme MegaCorp, in order
to create a more professional, regulated office environment,
issued a requisite office desk template to the employees,
dominated by gray. Manager #3 had approached Alan's desk.
"Alan, get rid of that purple tape dispenser! Aren't you a team
player?" At first, Alan objected, but he learned to adjust. That
was years ago.

When the Kleenex box with gray swirly designs on it ran out of
tissues, Alan purchased a Kleenex box with purple swirly designs
on it. Sitting in his ergonomic office chair, he contemplated the
box, words filling his mind:

> the purple vendetta
> dark eyes rolling down the highway
> big white spheres oozing down the eyeway
> revenge, recriminations, thick maroon fingers
> rubber-banding the pus of hurt onto a wall
> splattering a black bubbling tar
> full of scowling laughers and writhing snakes
> a purple neon shroud flashing off and on
> covering the brain, slipping off, re-adhering, slipping off
> a low dark rumble, sick spilling clouds
> and then daylight on the highway.

Manager #3 passed by Alan's cubicle and looked in. "Alan, is
that a purple Kleenex box? You know the rules." Alan reached
into his bag and got out an AK-47. It was painted bright yellow.

(originally published in *Unlikely Stories*)

Arnie Hippie

Arnie the aging hippie sat in his apartment in the Haight Ashbury district of San Francisco with Sprout Girl. "It's 'Kill Your TV' week!" he declared to Sprout Girl, who had been named Barbara at an earlier point in her life, but for many reasons, she was glad that she had synthesized a new identity as Sprout Girl. However, she was not sure that cohabitating with Arnie was a good idea. "The media tries to destroy our minds!" bleated Arnie, "But I won't let them!" While Sprout Girl agreed with some of Arnie's views about the media, she did not feel that all of television was inherently bad. Arnie lifted the Magnavox, as he had done with other televisions in previous years, and tossed it out the window to the ground, where it crashed in a hazardous spray of glass.

At that precise moment, Heather, just off the bus from Kansas, was ambling down the sidewalk barefoot, grooving on the freedom of being off the farm and on her own. In a haze of cosmic Cloud 9 stardust from her first LSD trip, Heather walked into the shards of broken glass from Arnie's TV, and let go with banshee howls. Arnie heard her and ran down the stairs, wracked with guilt. "Are you all right?" he asked as Heather continued to scream. "Look, I don't trust the medical establishment, but I know somewhere that can help," he said, referring to pseudo-Indian communities on Highway 43 that would handle things quietly, and heal her feet in a natural environment. Arnie helped Heather into the backseat of his 1967 Volkswagen Bus and headed toward Highway 43.

As she cleaned incense ashes from the coffee table, Sprout Girl recalled when, as Barbara, she had decided to tune in, turn on, and drop out, moving into Arnie's 'pad'. It had been an autumn evening in the suburbs, Barbara and her orthodontist husband were hosting a potluck with some of the other neighbors. Neighbor Husband #3 was talking about his orthodontic treatments, and Neighbor Wife #3 was commenting that this had an impact on the family popcorn hour, but that she had decided to be a good sport about it. Neighbor Husband #4 went on to describe the financial costs incurred to provide orthodontic treatment to 3 children, one of which compulsively chewed on tree bark in the backyard. Barbara inserted a well-positioned excuse into the general conversational flow (excuse=attend to a cooking appliance issue), dashed to the kitchen, and called Arnie, whom she had met at a protest. Within a month she was living in his apartment, changing her name to Sprout Girl.

But that was all in the past. The ringing phone roused Sprout Girl from her thoughts. It was Arnie, calling from the Volkswagen Bus. "Where's my trail mix? I expected to find trail mix in the elastic pocket on the driver's side door of the Volkswagen! We're on Highway 43, how does that look on the traffic channel?" There was a pause on the phone line, and then Arnie continued, "Oh yeah, I forgot, the TV's gone." Sprout Girl shrugged her shoulders and hung up the phone, soon deciding to leave Arnie and move on to a new life.

Arnie drove on, choosing to ignore the emissions spewed into the air by his Volkswagen Bus, as it was no longer within smog compliance standards. However, Heather had learned a thing or two about Volkswagen repair on the farm. This was only the beginning for Heather and Arnie.

(originally published in *Lit Up*)

The Plumfish

The plumtree is white today. The plumfish appeared in our garden as we sipped arsenic lattes in bucolic redwood chairs. A white newspaper emerged from the ground and wrapped itself around the flopping plumfish. As I prepared a strychnine au lait with our new espresso lifestyle coffee press, the plumfish moved out of the garden, and into our house, locking us out. Wrapped in the paper, it demanded preparation.

Channel 3

Sent out at fifteen to work in some hard-pressed house in the suburbs, Kay found Peter amongst the furniture she was dusting. He had a television remote in his hand and was clicking through the options. "I am channeling the spirit of Channel 3, so influential in my upbringing. 'The Banana Splits' and the 'Great Grape Ape' raised me from a sprout," he said as Channel 3 poured energy beams into his soul.

(originally published in *Short Fast and Deadly – Stolen Plums – stories required to open with one line from William Carlos Williams, and contain a reference to a type of fruit.*)

Reginald

Reginald had a walnut inside of his head. It had not been surgically inserted, he was born with it. The walnut gave him an intensified empathy for the problems of others, and voluminous knowledge on the cultivation of walnuts. However, one side effect of the walnut in his head was that it caused him to run out to his lawn every morning and sing opera for 10 minutes while spinning around on his side, burrowing a shoulder blade into the blades of grass.

Reginald's neighbors, disturbed by this behavior and its impact on adjoining property values, called an emergency homeowners association meeting to discuss the matter. In the meeting, which was particularly rambunctious as extra bubbles had been added to the complimentary carbonated soda, it was decided by well-meaning neighborhood representatives that the walnut should be removed from Reginald's head.

The next night, as he slept, the neighbors injected a sedative into his arm and transported him to a discount nocturnal surgeon. Reginald awoke the next morning and noticed that the walnut was gone, but found he no longer cared. He was referred by the neighbors to a therapist who helped him to see that his walnut-influenced thought patterns were abnormal, preventing him from fitting in. Reginald would no longer spin around on the lawn, mouthing opera. Instead, he found healthy socially-accepted alternatives for the weekend, usually revolving around the homeowners association.

He no longer had the intensified empathy for the problems of others, which some missed, but others found the new reduced level easier to be around. The Walnut Board terminated his employment, as Reginald could no longer provide his previously prolific amount of walnut information, but one of his neighbors found him a job in the town's paper mill and Reginald became a fully functional and well-liked part of the production line.

Reginald's neighbors enjoyed his new lifestyle for two years until one night in a dream Reginald saw a dark figure in a boat at sea. He had the same dream night after night, and the details became clearer. He was able to discern bags of walnuts in the boat, and the features of the dark figure resembled his own. When he woke up from the dream, Reginald found a mysterious walnut on his nightstand.

After 17 nights of this dream, and over 2 years of feeling at-sea, Reginald visited another surgeon, who re-installed the walnut in his head, much to the neighbors' consternation. Reginald again began to display the intensified level of empathy for the problems of others. He quit the paper mill, stopped attending homeowner association functions, and got reinstated to the Walnut Board, where he provided useful information for which he was paid well. He resumed spinning around on the lawn and bellowing opera, much to the dismay of his neighbors. Reginald knew that he had returned to his predestined path, meeting some like-minded walnut enthusiasts, and even a couple of alto lawn spinners.

The homeowners association and the neighborhood board decided to have more meetings about the non-compliant walnut trees in Reginald's yard.

(originally published in ***Ink Sweat and Tears***)

The Corporate Family

The sewing machines whirred in the factory division of Clothco Inc., hemming fabrics for the company's signature line of baby clothes. "We're all one big family here," said division manager Ryan loudly to his buddy the HR manager, as they walked along the sewing line. "That's the way it should be, like a row of obedient children," he added, smiling at the workers' heads that were turned downward. On the far wall, a gigantic mural of a jovial baby loomed overhead watchfully.

"I like your work, Enid," leered Ryan to one of the workers, giving her a pat on the behind as she returned to her sewing workstation, hurrying along to avoid his groping hands.

"She's a mousy one," laughed the HR manager.

"Make sure your beany's on tight, Enid, you know it's part of our corporate family dress code, now run along," added Ryan, watching Enid's timid, quiet countenance recede down the hall. All of the sewing machine workers were required to wear wired beanies on their heads, as a unique technology had been developed, in which the workers' suppressed rage could be harnessed through the wires into an energy force that powered the factory's sewing machines. The energy supplied would depend on the intensity of the rage.

Ryan returned to his desk and monitored the rage level of the sewing machines. Enid's level had reached that of nuclear Armageddon, according to the screen. "The meekest, quietest ones have the biggest volcano of pent-up rage," smiled Ryan. While Enid's rage level usually caused no real damage to be incurred by the durable Singer internals, this time her sewing machine started smoking, Enid's transmitted impulses of anger quickly shattering Ryan's monitor screen in explosive shards of glass, killing Ryan instantly.

Ryan's secretary Gwen found him slumped over, clutching his ball-point pen, blood dripping from his mouth. Being an efficient employee, Gwen felt conflicted about what to do next, since Ryan's report about corporate family morale needed to be completed as soon as possible. Thinking proactively, Gwen quickly snatched the report out from under Ryan's bleeding mouth and went to her desk to complete it, using some Liquid Paper to remove the blood stains. Upon completion, she forwarded it to the approvals department on time. Gwen then noticed Ryan, who was still slumped over at his desk, blood dripping into his 'Out Box'. She instructed the maintenance man to wheel Ryan, sprawled on his squeaky-wheeled ergonomically compliant office chair, to the basement, though the maintenance man felt that this was not part of his job description. Gwen made sure to attach a name tag to Ryan's shirt before he was wheeled away, as she knew that organizational skills were an important component of an efficient office.

A week later, in a company-wide meeting, the HR manager announced, "I see we have another body in the basement. As you know, we are one big family at Clothco Inc., and when a member of our employee family moves into the afterlife, we outfit for rebirth, ensuring enduring loyalty. Instead of wearing a suit in the coffin, we insist that a 'Clothco Inc' Funeral Diaper be worn! All employees will look quite snappy in that Funeral Diaper! It's the next step in eternal corporate casual attire!" Gwen and Enid looked up at the jolly baby smiling ominously on the large mural. After the meeting, the maintenance man had to attach the diaper to the corpse, again thinking this wasn't part of his job description, and bury Ryan's body near the parking lot.

Later that week, Enid and Gwen, now feeling like sisters in the corporate family, got together for lunch, and discussed what was to be done about the HR manager.

(originally published in *ppigpenn*)

My Neighbor Betty

*My neighbor Betty became my nemesis. I'm not sure how it all
began, but over the last 13 days, things escalated into an
intolerable state. Somehow I knew that today it would end,
resulting in the end of Betty or the end of me. I looked back at the
13 days, trying to figure out how it had gotten to this point.*

Day 1
The skate wheels turned as the animals glided about in our
neighborhood. "Arf-arf, meow-meow," the inserted tape
recorders brayed from inside the carcasses of the stuffed animals.
Betty's pet beagle was barking repeatedly, the tape was stuck.
They were filling the streets, gliding stuffed pets everywhere. I
saw Betty walking by, pulling a leashed television on wheels, a
dog being broadcast on the television screen. On the other side of
the street, Betty's husband Bill was running on a treadmill that
rolled along the pavement. Feeling neighborly, I offered to fix the
stuck audio tape in Betty's pet beagle, and she graciously
accepted the offer. However, I only succeeded in making it
worse, the tangled audio tape ending up strewn on the hot
pavement. I apologized to Betty and she laughed good-naturedly,
telling me not to worry about it, these things happen. As she
invited me and my wife Miriam to her house to play bridge, I felt
a shiver of darkness.

Day 2
Miriam and I went to Betty and Bill's house to play bridge. After
about 45 minutes, Betty brought out some baked goods from the
kitchen. She was always giving bread, pies, and cakes to the
neighbors. "I work at the bakery, so come by some time and I'll
get you a discount!" she said, setting raisin bread on the table,
returning to the kitchen for more. She brought out doughnuts,
muffins, biscuits, and croissants. It went on and on, the food
piling up on the table toward the ceiling. I asked Betty about her
stuffed pet beagle, and she pointed to the floor, where it lay with
some other stuffed animals. "Bill fixed the audio tape," said

Betty, pointing at Bill, hidden by the pile of baked goods. While daintily adjusting the little pink & red ribbons on the furry, cuddly stuffed bears & rabbits, Betty snarled, "Did you know that I stuffed these animals myself after bagging them? I skinned them, gutted them, and dried them. I have a full degree in taxidermy from the university!" The bridge game went on a few more minutes until Betty informed us that she had been to 'Rent-A-Smile' that day, but it had only been a six-hour treatment, and now the smile was starting to wear off.

Day 3
In the seafood chain restaurant lobby, Miriam and I noticed the velvet lobster, sitting in an unkempt tank amidst porcelain lead-lined tortoise shells, looking for a light of its Tareyton 100 cigarette. The tourists dropped their cigarette butts into the filthy water of the velvet lobster's tank. Not finding any other shellfish holding their lighters in sublime supplication, the velvet lobster busied itself with plans for the day. Looking at its shell-encrusted calendar, the velvet lobster noted that all its days for the next month were free, a good opportunity to pursue the 30-day weight loss program it had noticed on late-night television. The velvet lobster had used its little claws to somehow dial the phone and enroll in the 30-day weight loss program, though personally, the velvet lobster felt that it would take much less time to achieve its diet goal. Suddenly we saw our neighbor Betty enter the restaurant, pry the lobster out of the tank and throw it onto the floor. The velvet lobster made its way out of the restaurant, crawling past the occasionally-stuck double doors, into a nearby canal, where it achieved its 30-day weight loss goals. When we asked Betty why she did this, she yelled, "Mind your own business!"

Day 4
I went to Betty's house to ask about the velvet lobster. I approached the yard and saw two Doberman Pinschers. As one barked, a Technicolor bubble floated out of its mouth and into a nearby parking lot, attaching itself to the top of a car radio antenna. Both Dobermans kept barking, bubbles drifting out of their mouths. The bubbles eventually popped on the antenna of a

Dodge Dart at the northeastern edge of the parking lot. Looking out of the corner of my eye, I saw Betty's face in the window, screaming the word, 'ATTACK'.

Day 5
I went to the hospital for treatment of the wounds inflicted by Betty's Doberman Pinschers. Falling asleep in the waiting room, I woke up buried under a pile of dead bodies, flies buzzing overhead. The doctors and nurses twisted about spasmodically, stabbing each other with hypodermic needles. The intensive care patients on gurneys careened down the halls, out the double doors, and into the streets. They fell down manholes and floated through the sewer. I am negotiating my insurance bill.

Day 6
Returning home, and sensing more attacks from Betty, I phoned my Uncle Eugene, who was crafting porcelain weasels in his apartment and preparing an army of potted plants for battle. "My army of potted plants will strike via the element of **surprise!**" he said. "Now I'm not sure whether I need Philips Milk of Magnesia, or if I should be at the Philips 66 gas station located at the center point of Oklahoma, clipping the little weeds growing at the edge of its concrete service bay!" Uncle Eugene continued his observations, "There are those living the life of cloth puppets and brightly colored trousers in the rustic village boutique. They shut the door and large needle pins are stuck in all of us because the death of Kennedy had not been righted." I was beginning to doubt whether Uncle Eugene would be of much help.

Day 7
I went to Uncle Eugene's apartment to confer with him about Betty, though I still had my doubts about his effectiveness. In the lobby of the apartment building, I got into an elevator that was filled with pigeons. They were crapping all over the carpet. I was going to the fifth floor, and it was difficult to push the Number 5 button because the pigeons were obstructing the button console. The elevator was usually manned by an operator, but he had been subdued and covered by the pigeons. I saw his crumpled form in the corner of the elevator, his tattered gray uniform occasionally

appearing from under the pile of busily pecking birds. I eventually managed to push the Number 5 button and the elevator doors closed. The elevator slowly rose to the fifth floor as the pigeons cooed. Upon arrival on the fifth floor, the elevator doors opened and the pigeons flew out. A strange little man in a business suit appeared in front of the elevator doorway, demanding monetary compensation for the elevator operator's torn uniform. I chose to leave and took the elevator back down.

Day 8
I decided to observe Betty's specific actions over the next few days. She had been very open about displaying the activities of her household, and I took the opportunity to look into the window of their living room at night, searching for clues about her motivations. I saw Betty's husband Bill sitting in his Barcalounger with a seatbelt on. There was a parking meter next to the chair, and Bill was searching for change to put into the meter. An hour later, I saw Bill, in chinos and a polo shirt, exercising with an odd device of ropes and pulleys in his office, while Betty nearby putted a golf ball along a green Astroturf carpet, screaming orders of workout repetition on a megaphone: "56!....57!....58!......59!...."

Day 9
During the day, I managed to install advanced surveillance equipment in Betty's house, and was able to observe more activities: She sat her husband Bill down in front of the television, which was showing earnest young, black-leather-studded bands wearing long blonde wigs and warbling sheltered concern, while go-go dancers gyrated on top of giant orange cans of the diet cola that was sponsoring the program. "That should entertain him for a while," mumbled Betty, arranging stuffed animals around the room in a sort of occult death pattern. Later, Bill put his head into the oven, but was following the instructions of a cookbook, and didn't have enough ingredients.

Day 10
We looked across the fence at Betty's yard, seeing strange statues resembling baked goods, such as bread, cupcakes, and cinnamon

buns. Near the statues was a pile of dead rats. We saw Betty watering rhododendrons. "Hi, Neighbor! How's the yard doing, Betty?" we asked, trying again to be neighborly.

Betty sprayed more water on the rhododendrons. "Fine, though the rats are becoming a bit of a problem. Sorry about the Dobermans the other day," she said, holding a rat in her soil-stained hands, crushing it slowly.

"I hear the dead rats work well for composting, minerals for the soil, let's all recycle!" I said, glad that Betty was doing something about the rats.

"Thank you, have a nice day," said Betty, anxious to get back to watering her rhododendrons.

Day 11
My wife Miriam and I could feel the dark ways of Betty approaching. Miriam dabbled in vague tenets of Hinduism and had recently earned a degree in Mechanical Engineering at night school, specializing in the design of household appliances, particularly vacuum cleaners. She had a theory that she could vacuum Betty's bad karma out of her house, and she built a vacuum cleaner to do just that. "Leave it to me," said Miriam.

Day 12
I went to the bakery to buy a birthday cake for Miriam. A baking assistant was peering at me from behind loaves of bread. In one hand she held a butter knife and in the other hand a pair of scissors snapping menacingly. A saleswoman stepped up from behind the counter, clutching a riding crop and staring at me through binoculars, though I was only 8 feet away. She paced back and forth on the linoleum, striking her leg on alternate steps with the riding crop, screaming with pain and pleasure under the hot white bakery lights. I could see it was Betty, wearing a mask of the Pillsbury doughboy.

"Hello neighbor," I said.

"Enough frivolity and small talk," she hissed, pulling off the doughboy mask. As Betty prepared to strike me with the riding crop at the bakery, Miriam broke into Betty's house and vacuumed feverishly, sucking the bad karma into the bag.

Seconds later, I saw Betty's eyes fill with bliss and peace, the evil disappearing.

Day 13
Today I see Betty sitting in her backyard chaise lounge, staring at dead grass with a faraway look in her eyes, holding her stuffed velvet lobster. The vacuum bag was filled with bad karma and glowing menacingly, so Miriam contacted a hazardous waste removal team.

(originally published in *Defenestration*)

Toes

"They are so disturbing," she said, staring at his misshapen toes. Lottie and Sol were both 12 years old, and she was rejecting his footsie advances. It was a comment that would stick with Sol for years, causing him to develop a complex about his feet, for which he would compensate via career achievement as a podiatrist.

After years of study, Sol received numerous degrees related to the foot and started a practice. To advertise, he set up a large electric toe sign near the medical building in which he worked. After a typical day seeing patients, he sat alone in his office doing research, occasionally thinking about Lottie from his childhood who'd said his toes were disturbing, as the electric toe blinked on and off, casting a reddish light.

Lottie, meanwhile, became a professional bowler, though for her it was a lonely life, driving down bleak deserted highways to various tournaments, staying at desolate motels, often with no companionship except her bowling ball. When feeling extremely lonesome, she would set the bowling ball on top of the television set to keep her company, its finger holes resembling eyes, and its thumbhole looking like a little mouth. Lottie fought through the isolation and worked her way up through the rankings, succeeding on grit.

"Your toes went over the line, a foul!" screamed Lottie's competitor Lois during a crucial tenth frame roll. An argument ensued, and Lois angrily dropped a bowling ball on Lottie's foot. Showing steely resolve, Lottie went on to win the tournament but woke up the next morning with swollen and disfigured toes. The swelling eventually went down, but her toes remained permanently twisted, reminding her of Sol, that boy from her past.

Lottie began a comeback on the women's bowling circuit, rolling in small-money tournaments, though she was unable to find bowling shoes that would fit her bent toes and wrap comfortably around the contours of her feet. "I'm not going to let this stop me," said Lottie determinedly, clawing her way back to the top of the circuit, earning a finalist spot in the national championships in Las Vegas.

In Nevada for a podiatrist convention, Sol was channel-surfing in a hotel room as his crooked toes wiggled comfortably on a vinyl Ottoman. He tuned in to a bowling tournament and was amazed to see Lottie, rolling strike after strike. His heartbeat quickened when he learned that the bowling tournament was near the hotel.

The next day Sol sat in a lounge chair by the hotel pool, sipping a Mai-Tai, batting the little paper umbrella back and forth, watching the lounge chairs by the pool fill up with conventioneers and pro bowlers. Lottie's bowling nemesis Lois sat down in the lounge chair to Sol's left, and she tried to strike up a flirtatious conversation.

Lottie wandered over to the hotel pool after a strenuous practice session, relieved that her toes were no longer confined in bowling shoes. She sat on a lounge chair to Sol's right, and spread her tarsal digits freely in the summer air, slowly noticing the foot in the chair next to hers, a foot with the unforgettably contorted toes of Sol. Under the sun's glistening rays, Lottie rotated her foot to the left and made toe contact with Sol. When their feet merged, a lightning bolt sensation burst through their bodies, the toe friction transporting them into the cosmos. Lois recognized their bond, and slinked off scowling, to the tropical-themed bar.

Sitting by the fire, near his podiatry certificates and her bowling trophies, a half-century after their poolside encounter, Sol said, "They're looking a bit long, it's time for your trimming." Lottie smiled as Sol wielded the toenail clippers.

(originally published in *Linguistic Erosion*)

The Balloon Fiend

Willow drank a glass of water and saw purple kumquats dancing on the linoleum floor. "There's something strange in this water," she said, looking at the dripping tap over the kitchen sink.

"I'll write to the state's water commissioner about this!" she declared, sitting down at her desk. As she scribbled a letter, some green balloons wafted into the room. The balloons moved forward onto Willow and pressed her against a painting of sunflowers on the living room wall. One green balloon circled around the room, and then wrapped its string around her letter, lifting it off the desk and carrying it back out the window. At once, the other balloons released Willow and followed the first balloon out the open window.

The balloon with Willow's note floated across the city to the desk of Hiram, the state's water commissioner. Everything in Hiram's office was pale green, including Hiram, who was a fixture under fluorescent light. The balloons were participating in his project to taint the water supply and create more pliable citizens. "Well done!" said Hiram to the green balloon, rewarding it with a blast of helium, then reading Willow's note. "This citizen is becoming suspicious about the water supply," he announced to the other attentive balloons in front of his desk. "I want you to step up the surveillance." The balloons flew out the window, back toward Willow's house.

However, Willow had already left, speeding out of the city with her neighbor Julia towards the ocean. The balloons found and followed her car, which had a large sunflower painted on the roof. Trees, leaves, and sunlight flickered by as Willow and Julia accelerated through picturesque canyons. They arrived at a forest near the ocean and began exploring, as the balloons hovered nearby. Willow and Julia wandered along a path between moss-covered trees, emerging into a meadow filled with brightly colored flowers and butterflies, while the balloons continued their surveillance from above. The women played in the ocean waves and invited the balloons to join them. The balloons were hesitant at first, but soon were frolicking with Willow and Julia in the sea spray, drifting exuberantly through the foam, memories of Hiram collapsing into a misty collage of neon bubbles, melting together in the clear bright sunshine. The balloons became swirling lemonade lollipops bouncing through the saltwater waves amidst rising steam, as joy and exhilaration inflated them into the blue sky.

4 hours later, the balloons drifted peacefully back to the city. Each balloon was radiating a warm glow as it wafted into Hiram's office. He was sitting in a big pile of red balloons, enjoying the stinging sensation when one would pop. "Balloons, what's your report?!" demanded Hiram.

The balloons consulted amongst themselves, ready for freedom from Hiram's repressive control. "How about slowly pressing Hiram deep into the ground?" suggested one particularly aggressive balloon.

"No, it may ironically taint the city's water supply," replied another. Ultimately, the balloons decided to wrap their strings around Hiram's arms, and slowly lift him into the sky.

Willow and Julia looked up from the ocean waves to see the balloons and Hiram soaring into view. The balloons gently dropped Hiram into the surf, where Willow and Julia wrapped him in strands of seaweed and kelp. The balloons returned to the city and assumed new positions of responsibility.

(originally published in *MudJob*)

Office with an Ocean View

"I want to welcome everyone to the grand opening of our new corporate headquarters! We will make this company a top manufacturer of aquarium equipment!" said the CEO, Ben Aqua. There was a smattering of applause from the group of employees as the steel tower loomed above, casting a shadow over the oceanfront vicinity. AquaCo corporate headquarters was built near the ocean to afford majestic views for executives in select offices, despite a history of periodic tsunamis and flooding in the area.

Nobody was clapping louder than Debbie, who worked on the aquarium water pump assembly line. Due to her relentlessly cheery attitude and cutthroat maneuvering, Debbie would soon move up the ladder at AquaCo, to the position of Administrative Assistant for the Manager of Aquarium Gravel. "If we all work hard, then maybe we too can have an office with an ocean view, just like Ben Aqua!" said Debbie to some of her co-workers, who rolled their eyes, considering Debbie to be 'just another piranha in the tank'.

A few weeks later, the energy of the nearby ocean could be heard outside the steel tower as the Manager of Aquarium Gravel gave the status report to upper management. Upon finishing, he was elbowed in the ribs by his administrative assistant. "Tell them, tell them!" urged Debbie, brimming with excitement, clutching her manager's arm as a goldfish looked at them forlornly from its bowl.

"Ahem…" he said, "Well…with the help of my administrative assistant Debbie, we have come up with a bold new initiative to merge the Aquarium Gravel and Miniature Replica Castle divisions." There was a gasp in the room, not in response to the manager's proposal, but rather to the water that was suddenly rushing through the conference room doors. The ocean had risen and was starting to flood the 1st floor of AquaCo. Debbie was indignant that she and her manager wouldn't be able to make their presentation, which she felt would have propelled her career forward like a torpedo.

"Not to worry everybody, the water will let up," said Ben Aqua, gathering his papers amidst the onrushing kelp, and leading everybody upstairs to the 3rd floor. The flooding indeed stopped, but not before leaving the entire 1st level filled with water. "We'll make the 1st floor into an aquarium, I think that would be appropriate for AquaCo!" declared Ben Aqua in a flash of inspiration, as the ocean sound roared on the hallway speakers. Debbie nodded eagerly in agreement.

After the 1st floor was converted into an aquarium, Debbie often spent her lunch breaks staring through the glass windows at the swirling blue water and green seaweed. Late at night, she put on scuba gear and got into the 1st-floor aquarium, enjoying the immersion. She thought back to her childhood when she'd poured household cleaning solvents into her father's aquarium, killing his prized tetra fishes. "Debbie, don't you ever go near my aquarium again!" he'd screamed, his fish-like eyes bulging, "Stay out of my aqua life!" After an unspeakable disaster involving a Koi pond, Debbie's father would never speak to her again, but AquaCo was like a new family.

In her scuba suit, Debbie drifted peacefully through the aquarium water, thinking of her work family. Some of them, including Ben Aqua, were still at the office, working late. Looking outside through the window, she noticed the ocean waves growing larger, lapping at the side of the building. Suddenly the water roared in an onslaught independent of any organizational policy, and AquaCo was covered by the sea, the ocean reclaiming the landscape.

As she swam through the water-filled offices of AquaCo, Debbie looked fondly upon the drowned, bloated body of Ben Aqua in his office. "He was a great man, my 'work dad'!" she said chirpily from under the scuba mask, displacing him in his undersea ergonomic leather chair.

Debbie finally got that office with an ocean view.

(originally published in *Smashed Cat*)

Tennis and Lemurs

"Isn't she wonderful!" says Emma's mother to a friend, over drinks on the patio at the tennis club. On the tennis court nearby, Emma runs back and forth, returning tennis balls hit by a ball machine.

"Get to the ball quicker! Anticipate!" barks her instructor, Coach Snaff, as Emma lobs a shot across the net. Emma is showing great promise and has already won a number of junior tennis tournaments. As Emma completes the practice session with more forehands and backhands, a disturbance arises a few courts away.

Emma's mother turns and scowls at the approaching picket signs and angry voices. "Oh God, here they are again," she sighs. Recently, it had been discovered that the tennis club sits on the grounds occupied by the endangered spotted green lemur. Occasionally a spotted green lemur would cross a court during a match, evading the paths of speeding tennis balls, bewildering the players. Animal rights activists had soon learned of the situation and were out in force, protesting at the tennis club.

After the practice, Emma's mother calls, "Coach Snaff, may I have a word with you?" They descend the steps to his subterranean office, which resembles a bunker. "I don't want these protestors interrupting Emma's tennis trajectory!" seethes her mother, joining Coach Snaff at a surveillance camera monitoring the activists' movements. Coach Snaff has pictures of Hitler taped to the office's walls, as his childhood enthusiasms had been tennis and Der Fuehrer. Emma's mother looks approvingly at the decor as she unrolls charts and graphs on a table. "I have this current roadmap for Emma's tennis future," says her mother.

Coach Snaff's eyes brighten as he reviews the plan. "This reminds me of Hitler's forays into Poland," he enthuses while squeezing a tennis ball. Emma's mother looks at him, sensing a partner in darkness. Soon they are locking lips and tearing off clothes, squirming around in ecstasy as the scotch-taped Hitler photos detach from the wall in the heat, falling amidst writhing bodies in the devil's playroom.

Emma, who loves animals and actually wants to become a veterinarian, not a professional tennis player, stands outside, looking on sympathetically at the animal rights activists, who are holding up signs depicting spotted green lemurs at play. She puts tennis balls into the ball machine, and somewhere within, starts to hear her own voice.

They emerge from the bunker onto the tennis court, shouting threateningly at the protesters. "You're not going to derail my daughter's tennis career over a lemur!" yells Emma's mother. A few angry tennis club employees want to physically confront the activists and the lemurs. That sounds good to Coach Snaff and Emma's mother. "Get over here Emma, it's time to hit some overhead smashes!" orders Coach Snaff.

"Do as we say, Emma, get over here!" Emma turns on the ball machine, slowly aiming it at her mother and Coach Snaff, pelting them with tennis balls, a real smile finally appearing on her face.

(originally published in *Short Humour*)

The Plastic Suitcase

The little boy sat by the pond, tousled hair in his eyes, feeling the cool grass between his toes, smiling as he looked at the fish swimming in the water. It was a pond from Steve's childhood.

Steve was awoken from his dream by a shrill ring of the cell phone. "We require your services at corporate immediately. Catch the next plane out," said the voice on the phone line. Steve put plastic clothes into a plastic suitcase. He put a plastic toothbrush onto plastic teeth, brushing with even strokes.

Zoom, Zip, Bang! Steve thrust himself into the synergy of the moment. "Give me a plastic Pina Colada, baby, I'm here to stay!" he said to the flight stewardess. He whispered sweet nothings into the ear of the other stewardess, who was splayed out upon the plastic food tray, delighting in the peanuts, Sprite, and napkins that were sucked into her writhing spray-shellacked beehive hairdo nudging itself against the industrial tan fabrics of the reclining seat in the preceding row, occupied by the portly businessman.

Steve's plane landed at the airport and he walked through the plastic terminal, staring forward with a steely glint, checking his media devices, texting appropriate responses. After looking at his plastic agenda for the corporation's ball-bearing and therapy advertising campaign, he got into the new rental car, air conditioning on, friendly fumes of lacquer and paint solvents filling his lungs. The temperature, as always, was 68 degrees Fahrenheit.

When he arrived at corporate headquarters, the employees flung themselves at his feet, kissing his hard plastic boots, their lusting eyes craving his image. Steve entered the conference room, where his team showed him charts and graphs. The team milled about, commenting, pursuing deep-seated needs, hoping to find an advantage and gain Steve's favor, carrying out Freudian agendas as they acted upon the murky volcano lurking deep within their unconscious. Later, Steve and the management team bonded over martini olives, brilliantly reforming the ball-bearing and therapy advertising campaign into a cultural force.

Steve woke up the next morning, writhing amongst the secretaries on plastic sheets in the plastic bed, administrative lacquered plastic fingernails slicing thin rivulets of blood into his back. Festive, hunching orangutans flew through the dark spaces of the hangover in his skull, while he prepared his mind for the next gathering of hard-charging entrepreneurs, looking to create a new tomorrow for the rest of us, little grey monkeys trimming nails from their bulging toes. Steve decided to step outside and walk around the ponds and rivers of the corporate grounds.

He saw the little boy sitting in the grass by the pond, still smiling at the fish in the water. The boy waved to Steve, and Steve waved back, seeing himself from long ago. Sadness and regret started to overwhelm him. He blinked and the boy faded away, waving goodbye.

Steve regrouped and looked at the water, deciding that there weren't enough fish. "What about piranha? What about carp?" he demanded. Steve got on the phone and decided to make things happen, placing a call to facilities, with a dictum of restocking corporate's plastic ponds and rivers with piranha and carp.

His coup at corporate complete, Steve packed his plastic suitcase and left headquarters for the next assignment, located in a climate where he was sure to find more succulent piranha and carp. Instead, he'd find blood on a broken air conditioner, a story that would end with hard nails in a warm room.

(originally published in *Farther Stars Than These*)

Quack

Bill sat on an overstuffed chair full of feathers, beaks, guts, spleens, stomachs, livers and eyes. He could hear chirping and quacking emanate from the chair. He was in his den clicking the television remote control, finally choosing Channel 38 University of the Air, Sky and Galaxy. On the screen, a man was sitting at a wooden desk in front of a blackboard in a stark room. Suddenly the man at the desk and the blackboard disappeared in a big ball of light filling the television screen. "Bill!" it roared, "you are not what you think you are, you are a stream of energy coursing through a body, a vessel, a shell. You are like me!" said the ball of light.

The quacks and chirps from the chair got louder and Bill snapped, "Ssshh birds, I'm trying to watch this!" As he uttered those words, the ball of light disappeared from the television screen, and the man reappeared at the desk, hitting the blackboard with a steel pointer and quacking. Bill then slowly murmured, "Hello birds, thank you for letting me enjoy your vessels. When my vessel has deconstructed into a new form, and its pieces fly off in shards of flame, I hope you will enjoy the use of it, just as I have enjoyed the use of yours."

The chirping and quacking continued from the chair as the ball of light returned to the television, saying, "Yes, you are just a stream of energy from the universe."

Bill's wife Norma was in the kitchen with their niece, cooking chicken. Norma heard the commotion and entered the den, where she was alarmed by her husband's appearance. "Bill, you look like you had too many of those 99 cent vitamin packets from the 7-11," she said in a concerned tone, looking at the array of brochures on the coffee table. "Have you been reading more of those New Age transcendence pamphlets?"

"No dear, I'm fine," said Bill, staring at a picture of mallards on the den's fine-wood-grain-paneled wall.

"We have enough problems just trying to pay the bills, without your excursions into metaphysical whatnot," said Norma, leaving the room as Bill slowly transformed into a bright ball of light.

When Norma returned to the den, Bill was gone, and on the television screen was a duck, sitting at the desk in front of the blackboard. "Now listen to me, Norma," said the duck. Norma tried to use the remote clicker, but the television was stuck on Channel 38. "You have enjoyed our vessels, though we are all really one with the universe. Quark-Quark! I mean Quack-Quack!"

The duck on the television insinuated itself into her being, its webbed feet grabbing hold. It pecked at Norma's conscience, hunting for niblets of corn inside the inner reaches of her cortex gray matter, perching on a cactus of thought beneath the blue shine of her inner cranium. The duck's bill pecked urgently, as Norma was transformed into a bright ball of light, joining Bill in a new consciousness, in tune with the cosmos.

Bill and Norma's molecules seemed to have disappeared from the neighborhood, though it was rumored that they were still in the vicinity. Their niece went to the park's duck pond every week, to sit and listen to the quacking.

(originally published in *Linguistic Erosion*)

The Neighbors and the Vole

The vole is a secret agent, scuttling along the perimeters of suburban housing developments, observing behavior patterns of inhabitants. The vole accumulates data and reports it to higher authorities at Yardtel Inc., a multinational corporation with feelers in the area.

When the Sneedwillows move into the neighborhood, the vole goes on high alert, seeking stimuli, its nose sniffing at sidewalks, fences and patches of mulch. Yardtel Inc. develops increasingly sophisticated technology and equips the vole with cutting-edge surveillance tools, which the vole employs efficiently to gather new information. Busybody neighbors meanwhile utilize highly complex binoculars and cameras to observe the vole and the Sneedwillows. The vole and the busybody neighbors keep each other under constant surveillance.

Now ensconced in the neighborhood, Mrs. Sneedwillow, wearing a bright red dress, trims edges of the front lawn minutely with tweezers each day, then returns to the house. On Saturdays, Mr. Sneedwillow, wearing a bright green tuxedo, mows the lawn, grass clippings affixing themselves to his outfit. Various relatives visit, dressed in bright blue, while assorted friends stop by, all dressed in bright yellow. The neighbors are baffled by the Sneedwillows, and continue their observation, as does the vole. The vole notices that Mr. Sneedwillow has purchased, at great expense from a catalog, a serenity pod, a bed shaped like a large porcelain egg, replete with relaxing music and soothing vibration. This looks very appealing to the vole.

One day, a red hearse pulls up, and Mrs. Sneedwillow is loaded in, while Mr. Sneedwillow sheds tears into a bright green handkerchief. A week later, Mr. Sneedwillow passes away. Both of the Sneedwillows are buried in the front yard. The vole informs Yardtel Inc. of the developments, and it purchases the yard in a yard sale, along with the garage, in a garage sale.

One of Yardtel's subsidiaries is the cable Tyrant Channel. Using the yard as an advertisement resource, the corporate interests of Yardtel, Inc. plant posters of Hitler, Stalin, Mao and Pol Pot on the front lawn, and bring in a mysterious cloaked figure to mow the grass at 4 a.m., carving a Hitler mustache into the grass. As neighbors voice objections to the signs, a slow greenish red liquid seeps up from the ground near the Sneedwillows' well-manicured gravesites. It curdles into a strange pool that dissolves Hitler's lawn mustache, and spreads through the lawn, pulling the tyrant posters down into the ground.

Not seeing a revenue upside to the situation, Yardtel Inc. sells the yard to the cable Hedge Channel, which uses lawn clippers to convert the greenery into a miniature labyrinth, enjoyed by local mice and squirrels.

The vole, upon reviewing the latest developments, has what can be termed as a crisis of conscience. It decides to retire, buying a serenity pod and then spending most of its time in the porcelain egg. The neighbors become bored with viewing the vole in its serenity pod, so they observe and record each other instead, looking forward to reporting it somewhere.

(originally published in *Short Humour*)

Lima Beans

Sally looked at the pile of lima beans on her plate. "I don't like this food, why do I have to eat it?"

"Be quiet and eat your lima beans, or you'll go to your room." said her mother.

At the bean conference in Lima, Ohio, a single lima bean was on a small table in the middle of the auditorium, under a harsh white light. "We all must eat the town bean," yelled the crowd.

"But I don't want to!" responded a small child, who was quickly removed from the room by security.

"The lima bean's origins are in Lima, Peru," asserted a woman in a pea-green sundress, and there were roars of agreement throughout the auditorium.

A man in a severe yellow suit disagreed, arguing that the bean came into existence in Lima, Ohio, and was somehow linked to former pro golfer Tony Lima (one of only 3 two-time winners of the Buick Open). There was some angry murmuring in the room about the Tony Lima theory when a steaming vat of lima beans was wheeled into the auditorium, and all participants consumed one bean apiece.

"Will this help resolve the disagreement about the origin of the lima bean?" the leader of the bean conference asked the briefly munching throng.

The answer was a resounding "No!" as eating this bean with broad pods put each person into an even fouler mood, and the debate about the lima bean became more rancorous and unproductive.

The man in the severe yellow suit arose once again and announced, "I am one of the kumquat people!" Half the auditorium roared cheers, joining the man in a chant of "We are the kumquat people!"

The other half of those in the auditorium yelled in response, "We are the bean people!"

"Why didn't you buy the lima beans at the discount mart instead of that strange health food emporium?" asked Sally's mother in the kitchen.

Sally's father took a deep breath and loosened his yellow tie, saying, "The discount mart didn't have the kumquats I like, but that 'strange' health food emporium did."

>*The bean people came from pods, but that was their only 'abnormality'. In every other aspect, they were exemplary citizens, living life on the low burner of the universal gas stove. Some had been through tumultuous incarnations, and were ready for peaceful conformity, following rules that were the bedrock of their bean-oriented society.*
>
>*The kumquat people had been crawling from their caves for centuries, agitating the bean people. "We bring revolution!" screamed the kumquat people, thumping their golden orange citrus tomes.*
>
>*The bean people countered, "We shall slay you and your heretical ideas!" while fist-pounding their corresponding legume scriptures.*

Sally's mother rolled her eyes. "You know we need to save money, Sally needs new clothes for school. Why can't you be responsible? Am I the only adult here?"

"I'm going to buy more kumquats tomorrow!" yelled Sally's father.

>*The leader of the bean conference announced, "I believe that no resolution will be met at this time about the origin of the lima bean, nor about the merits of lima beans vs. kumquats."*
>
>*The man in the severe yellow suit added, "There seemed to be no discord at all until that little child refused to eat the town bean, and had to be removed from the room. That's when the trouble started!" He looked to the woman in the pea-green sundress, and she nodded her slight approval, eliciting his relieved sigh.*

"Yes, it's the child's fault that we disagree!" yelled the crowd.

"Well Sally, that's a nice little story about kumquat and bean people, but you still can't have any kumquats until you finish the lima beans," said her mother. Sally scowled at her plate, and her parents resumed arguing.

(originally published in **Linguistic Erosion**)

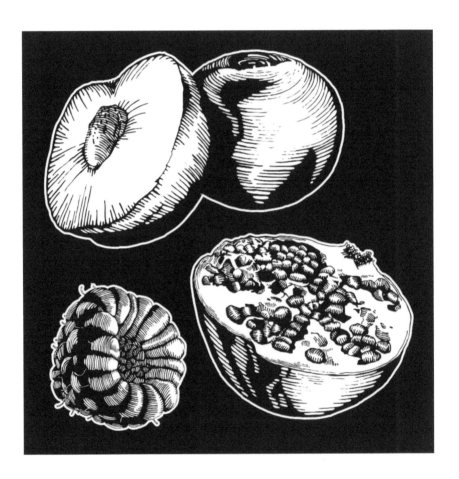

The Soul of Perry

"Oink-oink-oink!" sang Perry, happy that a multimillion-dollar megamerger had just fallen into place, generously expanding the portfolios of influential stockholders. "Snort, snort, orngk," he grunted, as the little green numbers rolled across the screen, nothing but good news. Perry jumped off the swivel chair into the little mud pit below his desk, rolling, grunting, squealing, much to the approval of his secretary, Miss Ladentas, who stood looming over Perry's mud pit, her shadow casting a pall over the proceedings, blocking out the dim hazy sun framed by the Manhattan skyline.

"You've done it again, Perry, now sign these," said Miss Ladentas darkly, shoving a pile of contracts into Perry's mud pit, and he pressed his little hoof into each one earnestly, knowing that his signature guaranteed economic fortune.

Perry still sat in the mud but was starting to stomp his little hoof in more haphazard directions. "Oink…flowery paisley sunshine redwood consciousness, happy little madmen spreading their magic wands," he blurted. Apparently, Perry's slop had been altered inadvertently by the young man from the mail room, leaning over Perry's desk to deliver microfilmed documents, a tab of hallucinogen tumbling out of his shirt pocket.

Perry trotted out of the building and hopped a cab to Central Park, arriving at a meadow where he instinctively knew where to dig up a little magical uniform. He slipped, squirmed, and slid into the uniform, rainbow colors expanding around him.

Miss Ladentas knew that the situation was getting out of control. Perry was no longer of use. A pity, as he had shown such promise. He was now out-of-bounds and could not be reined in. "It's a shame that some are not meant to realize the great potential for which they are called," she thought to herself, as a flower child uptown painted Perry's hooves bright purple. However, Elaine Ladentas would go on to bigger things.

Years later, Perry was on the bus headed towards the presidential palace. Along the highway were billboards, each one singing the praises of Elaine the Dictator. "Unity=Prosperity!" spouted one, displaying child laborers on a hillside, all wearing boxy shorts, hoeing the dirt merrily. Somehow this woman who had once been his secretary was now dictator of the country. Perry was one of the random citizens chosen to participate in a much-photographed sojourn through the bowels of Elaine's government, the tour having been carefully pre-planned by the authorities. "Elaine's home is your home!" screamed the words in the mandatory pamphlet he was reading.

Upon entering the palace, Perry walked along with the procession, following a yellow dotted line bounded by red velvet ropes, as actors recreated triumphant scenes from Elaine's dictatorship. While viewing a reenactment of a military coup being crushed, Perry tripped on a bump in the carpet, tumbling over the velvet ropes and through an adjacent door, into the bathroom of Elaine the Dictator.

She sat in a tub at the far end, staring vacantly at mists of steam rising from the water, a ceremonial pile of ice slabs in the middle of the room. The colorful turned-on vibrations from Perry's soul rose to battle the muddy black pit of Elaine's consciousness, the psychic energies colliding, first creating a ball of light, then a slowly evolving 'Chia Pet' on the tile floor of the bathroom, a little ceramic pig with green sprouting seeds, a devil baby.

Elaine glanced at the ceramic pig and decided that this was not a manifestation of her spiritual goals. She quickly vacated the premises on all physical and metaphysical levels. Perry moved into the palace but soon found that he missed Elaine, who had ruled the country with an iron fist and deadly force until encountering the sunshine soul of Perry.

(originally published in *Clockwise Cat*)

Hoover Dam

Neda worked in a gift shop at the edge of the Hoover Dam in 1936, selling small dam replicas to tourists. Her beloved, a pioneering biologist named Dane, had disappeared while researching Gila monsters in the desert. Neda's tears for her missing sweetheart dripped upon the postcards of the Hoover Dam in the gift shop, smearing the images of sky and cement. Most tourists would not buy the postcards in that condition, though some art-inclined visitors felt that the tears added a new dimension to the otherwise humdrum depiction of the Depression-era water-damming edifice, paying extra dollars and cents for a postcard abstracted by the fluid of Neda's tear ducts.

One morning, a 4-year old hellion named Edna ran amok in the gift shop, knocking trinkets off the shelves, tearing up reprinted images of the dam. A frustrated Neda slapped a decal of the Hoover Dam to Edna's forehead, angering Edna's influential parents, resulting in Neda being fired later that morning. Little Edna soon enjoyed a lunch of toast and herbal tea, but Neda did not have as pleasant a meal, munching on difficult wafers, blood and regrets.

That night, feeling lost without Dane, Neda walked along the length of the Hoover Dam, holding a metal fork in the air in the midst of a lightning storm, waiting for a shock from above. Neda received the jolt 2.8 minutes into the walk, being struck down by the fatal jagged bolt of light, spasmodically clutching the kitchen fork as the volts worked their way through her skeleton and membrane. After her death, the local legend was that Neda's spirit still trolled the desert in a 1934 Studebaker, pining for her lost love Dane.

Two decades later, the child from the gift shop, Edna, having grown up, had a baby in Kingman, AZ. The baby had a strange rectangular birthmark on her forehead. During her pregnancy, Edna had been feeling a strong pull toward the Hoover Dam, seeing it in the kitchen sink water reflection, and as a shape mysteriously mowed into her lawn, a sort of small-scale suburban 'crop circle'.

One night storm clouds gathered over the desert, and Edna could no longer resist the pull. She packed the baby into her 1954 Studebaker and drove along the highway toward the Hoover Dam. As she neared the dam, Edna saw a broken down car by the side of the road, with a Gila monster near its right front tire. Alone in the car was an infant, apparently abandoned. Edna pulled to the side of the road to rescue the deserted child, placing him next to her baby in the back seat. In Edna's Studebaker, the two infants, reincarnated souls of Neda and Dane, locked eyes as lightning struck in the desert.

Edna drove to the local authorities, and after weeks of investigation and paperwork, was able to adopt the baby she had found in the abandoned car. The two infants were inseparable, growing together into childhood, then adulthood. As the years went by, they pooled together enough money to buy the Hoover Dam gift shop, which they would run together throughout eternity.

(originally published in *Daily Love*)

Monopoly

Victor sat down for a game of Monopoly with some of his friends from the stock firm. After a few rolls of the dice, Victor noticed that Marvin Gardens had been replaced by Forest Oak Road, his street, on the game board, occupied by an iron, shoe, hat, and plastic green house. Bewildered by this turn of events, Victor stepped outside for a breath of fresh air. In front of his property, he saw a cast iron 5-foot tall shoe, a large iron hat, and a small green cottage that seemed to be built from an exotic variety of twigs.

Victor pressed his nose against the one lone window of the cottage, and encountered a vision of orange $500 bills, grandiose 'Community Chests', and strangely dancing 'Chance' question marks. The green cottage reminded him of one of his past financial coups, a small green orphanage. Victor had succeeded in leveraging this asset for sizable profits. The orphans were removed, some ending up on the slums of Baltic Ave.

Victor decided to walk further down the street, where he saw a Stop sign that read 'DO NOT PASS GO, DO NOT COLLECT $200'. He turned away from the sign and crossed the railroad tracks, where he was hit by the oncoming Short Line Railroad. Floating into unconsciousness, Victor eventually woke up in the big red hotel. But this hotel was not on the Boardwalk, it was under the Boardwalk, way under, on fire. And no room service was available.

(originally published in *Postcard Shorts*)

Mr. Enzyme

"Bill, what I like about you is your predictability, I always know what I'm going to get from you, and that's hamburgers," said Bill Pleck's neighbor nemesis Gene, peering over the fence as Bill barbecued hamburgers in the back yard on a summer's evening.

Suddenly Bill Pleck tore off his barbecue apron and threw it down in disgust, stomping on it emphatically. Next, he poured lighter fluid on the apron, torched it, and reached into a shopping bag, removing a chef's apron, on which was lettered 'Mr. Enzyme'. "An enzyme is a chemical catalyst, an agent of change, and that's what I will be! My new name is Mr. Enzyme, no matter what people say, even you!" he declared, gesturing toward Gene, whose eyes were glued to a pair of binoculars, focusing on the briquettes in the barbecue.

"I'm not pleased by this change in apron habits," said Gene.

Mr. Enzyme approached his wife Barbara with his new plan for change. They both agreed that their lives up to this point had been unsatisfyingly predictable. Feeling ready for something new, Barbara agreed to a new identity as Mrs. Enzyme. They each talked of redefining their past. "I've decided that I've had a mysterious past in smoke-filled Mahjong dens," said Mrs. Enzyme, staring wistfully into the distance.

"And I've had a past as a proprietor of a seedy motel on the outskirts of Los Angeles!" said Mr. Enzyme.

Their next action was to remodel one half of their house into a pink castle in the image of her childhood dollhouse, and modify the other half into a dark oak wood old British men's club motif that he preferred. ("As part of our redefinition, we'll also mix the two styles together, so as not to be restricted by gender roles!" said the Enzymes) As the workmen started demolishing one of the rooms of the house to convert it into a garish purple and pink puppet theater, and part of the green pastel kitchen was wrecked to make room for vigorous espresso-toned enclaves, neighbor Gene approached the house, chunks of concrete tumbling down around him. "Look Enzyme, or whatever you're calling yourself now, there's a building code!" said Gene, who was a rising player in the Homeowner's Association.

"We're within the building code, Gene," said Mr. Enzyme, showing him the paperwork. As Gene stalked away, Mr. Enzyme called, "See you this weekend at the neighborhood pot luck!"

On the evening of the pot luck, Mr. Enzyme proudly brought forward the chicken wings from his barbecue, displayed appealingly on a platter. Gene moved forward, challenging Mr. Enzyme's pot luck offering. "What's your game, Enzyme? I usually bring the chicken wings to this shindig, you usually cook hamburgers."

"This is a part of our redefinition, Gene," said Mrs. Enzyme, standing by her husband, letting her natural gravitas weigh in on the situation.

As the evening progressed, the neighbors showed an overwhelming preference for the Enzymes' chicken wings, leaving Gene's wings untouched. "We can be anybody we want to be, Gene," said the Enzymes, munching on potato salad. "It's a perspective on reality, a choice you can make."

"But you can't run away from who you really are. You're Bill and Barbara Pleck, you cook hamburgers!" insisted Gene.

"Or maybe we're beings in constant change, not everybody's the same," said the Enzymes.

Gene stared at them for a long time but had nothing to say. He picked up his chicken wings and went home, as the Enzymes slowly morphed into green lizard aliens, their protruding tentacles inspecting the coleslaw

(originally published in *Linguistic Erosion*)

The Elevator

"3rd-floor souls, Hardware and Lawn Care!" announced the department store elevator operator, a round jovial man with twinkling eyes and a mischievous grin. Helen and her husband Don were in the elevator, carrying boxes of hats.

Looking at Don from under her floppy hat, Helen said, "I had a dream that I was in a lobby of 400 elevators, each a different color. Every few seconds, I hear the ping of one of the elevators, and I run toward its open doors, which slam shut as soon as I reach them. Then another elevator pings, I run toward its doors, they slam shut, and so on. So I keep missing the doors, but in the dream, I'm learning how to miss the doors in style. My therapist says that all this has to do with issues of abandonment. What do you think, Don?"

Don hadn't heard her, as his mind was filled with visions of green grass, fertilizers, sprinklers, and various lawn care responsibilities. "It's not sensible to have so many hats," he said, looking at Helen's hat boxes.

He set the boxes down in the elevator, and stepped out onto the 3rd floor of the department store, suddenly finding himself in the middle of a large expanse of grass. A woman in a blue tunic rode across the lawn on a riding mower, waving to him. "Join me on the mower, Don!" she yelled cheerily, "Adventure awaits!"

"You missed a spot," said Don, pointing to a patch of un-mowed grass, as the woman in the blue tunic rode the mower around in circles.

"Good observation, Don," said the round jovial elevator operator with the mischievous grin, his twinkling eyes cutting through Don. Helen looked on without much regret as Don boarded the riding mower, deserting her in the elevator as the doors closed.

On the next floor, a man in a yellow tunic entered the elevator and picked up one of Helen's hat boxes. "Get your hands off of that," ordered Helen promptly, slapping him with a fly swatter she had bought in the 'House Wares' section. The man in the yellow tunic wasn't bothered so much by the fly swatter itself but did not enjoy the swats of the hard plastic coating package containing it. Nevertheless, he continued to eye the hats with great interest.

The elevator stopped at each floor, but Helen did not disembark, as the level of her soul had not been reached. "Your soul's floor is the roof," said the elevator operator jovially, his twinkling eyes cutting through her. Upon reaching the roof, the elevator doors opened upon a sweeping, colorful sky. The man in the yellow tunic led Helen onto the top of the building. As she stared at an airplane in the sky, she flashed back to when she was 8 years old, waving to her parents on the runway as they boarded their flight, her mother in a floppy hat, her father wearing a fedora, hours before they would disappear from her life in a plane crash.

"Hey, we love your hats," said the people on the roof, all in yellow tunics, admiring the contents of Helen's hat boxes.

"You're the first people who have appreciated my accumulation of hats," she declared, gratefully. Earlier in the day, she had a session with her therapist, who told her that she was buying too many hats.

In the rooftop community, Helen instantly became known, and thrived as 'The Hat Lady'.

(originally published in *Linguistic Erosion*)

Soul Bowl

Milo worked at the bowling alley, troubleshooting problems with the ball-return machines, shelving the bowling balls at the end of the night and performing various maintenance duties. Until a couple of weeks ago, he had been an accountant in the big city. Suddenly Milo quit his job at the accounting firm, left the city, and started working at the bowling alley in a nondescript town. Milo loved working at the bowling alley, as the crash of pins seemed to trigger various pleasant memories in his subconscious.

About six months before, while still working as an accountant, Milo had started slipping into strange bowling-related trances. When visiting a museum, he would enjoy contemplating the fire extinguisher on the museum wall, as it seemed to resemble a large bowling pin. The blackberries, plums, cherries, and tomatoes in still-life and landscape paintings also soon represented, to Milo, nothing but multi-colored bowling balls.

Milo had decided to see a psychiatrist about his bowling obsession. On his first visit, while looking at the diplomas and certificates on the wall, Milo couldn't help noticing the bowling trophies that were situated about the doctor's office in a pattern that he found hostile and aggressive. The psychiatrist had launched into a pseudo-Freudian theory involving penis envy, indicating that bowling pins represented an unconscious compensation by Milo for a small endowment. Milo emphatically rejected this theory and had stopped seeing the psychiatrist.

As he stacked bowling shoes at the alley, Milo answered his cell phone, which had a ringtone of crashing bowling pins. It was his former boss from the accounting firm, Maura. "Milo, we need you back here at the firm, let's talk tomorrow," said Maura. Milo began to answer but slipped into a pleasant reverie upon hearing the 16 lb. bowling balls roll along the maple wood. He clicked his cell phone off.

The next day, Maura approached Milo at the bowling alley as he was excavating a stuck Brunswick from a malfunctioning ball return machine. "Why Maura, what a surprise!" exclaimed Milo, knowing that she would appear sooner or later. "Let's talk while I work," said Milo as he completed toiling on the ball return machine, and proceeded to lie down on a bench in the bowling area, reaching underneath to tighten screws and hinges that had come loose.

Maura pulled up a green plastic chair, "Milo, I don't understand why you left the office to work here..." started Maura, but her voice trailed off as she began to feel the hypnotic effect of the bowling alley: the crashing pins, the balls rolling on wood, the chatter throughout. Milo looked on knowingly as Maura slipped off into a bowling-induced trance, where images of her childhood in the suburbs drifted into her mind....*There were aquamarine swimming pools situated in the backyards of houses with pastel automobiles parked in front, rubber tires lodged against the heated summertime asphalt. 11-year old Maura and her friends were in a bowling league. She loved the air conditioning at the bowling alley in the hot summer...she wanted to be there forever...* Maura awoke refreshed hours later in the parking lot, as Milo had brought her outside for some fresh air.

Within days, Maura quit the accounting firm and got a job at the bowling alley where Milo worked. As she and Milo took a cigarette break out in the parking lot, a large family was walking back to their car from the sporting goods store, most of the children clad in Little League baseball uniforms, when one of the non-uniformed kids, an 11-year old girl named Marcia, felt drawn towards the bowling alley, near Milo and Maura. "This is for me, I'm home," said Marcia dreamily, as the parents looked on in alarm, but oddly yielding.

Maura and Milo reached for her hand, saying, "Come closer child, follow us." And she did.

(originally published in *Daily Love*)

Keys

Where are my keys? Burt was in his office on the 31ˢᵗ floor, looking for his keys. They were not in his pants pockets or his briefcase. He looked in every drawer of his desk, under the rug, up in the ceiling light fixtures. He pulled pictures of mallards off the walls, but the keys weren't behind them! He overturned his desk and tore up the plaid cushions of the office couch. Soon the entire office was in a shambles. "Hmm…where could they be?" Burt said to himself. He took out an axe and hacked holes in the walls, searching through the building structure for his keys.

Burt could not find his keys in the office, so he walked down the hall to the elevator, maybe his keys were in the car. There was an elevator operator he had never seen before. "Hello Burt, I am Mr. Pelican," he said. "Join me in the elevator, which will take us to the stars. I had the nape of my neck shot off in the war, but I still lead a productive existence as 'Your Host on the Elevator'. You quiver, you shake, but don't worry, Burt, all will be copasetic." Burt looked at the elevator operator suspiciously, just wanting to get to the ground floor and look for his keys in the car. The elevator door closed and the suspended cage descended to the 13ᵗʰ floor, its door opening to reveal a corridor. "All the doors in the corridor are closed, but behind each one is a key to the evolution of your soul. You will now have the opportunity to choose a door, Burt," said the elevator operator. "One of the doors may yield immeasurable enlightenment and joy, but another door may lead you down a dark road from which there is no return. So there is a risk, but also an opportunity for spiritual growth. Which door do you choose?" he asked.

"Just take me to the lobby, I want to get to my car," said Burt.

Where are my keys? Burt arrived at the ground floor and checked the car, but his keys were not there. He decided to walk down the street and through a park towards a nearby locksmith. In the park, he stopped by a pond to stare at the ducks. The clouds above were speeding by as Burt suddenly felt tired and drifted off to sleep, dreaming of walking down endless corridors and opening locked doors. When Burt awoke, he saw a pelican in the pond, clutching a key in its beak, saying, "Burt, this is your chance to open the door."

Burt ran to the office building and found the elevator operator. "I want you to take me back to the 13th floor!" he exclaimed, telling Mr. Pelican about his dream and what he'd seen in the pond. "But first, tell me what this all means! What doors do I need to open?"

"What do you want it to mean?" replied Mr. Pelican, handing over Burt's missing keys, informing him that the building never had a 13th floor.

(originally published in *Short Humour*)

Pools

The house we bought in a picturesque canyon was an underpriced bargain, the previous owner desperate to sell. It was cavernous and we would never have enough furniture to fill it. The canyon winds swirled through its halls. There was a large empty pool in the backyard, lined with cracked cement, vines crawling around the grey interior, a dried-out diving board perched over the deep end. There seemed to be an alluring bleakness to the empty pool.

We set about restoring the pool to its original condition. While dealing with the cement contractors, I found a wadded-up piece of paper at the bottom of the dry pool. On the wad of paper were the chlorine-stained words 'Dead Pool Scrolls'. I could not decipher the rest of the water-smeared words and deposited the paper in a desk drawer, where it was soon forgotten.

The pool was restored, and we enjoyed evenings in the water, as whippoorwills and hummingbirds flew above. In the summer, we went on vacation and returned to find that our neighbor to the south, Bill Poseidon, had, in the name of neighborhood sociability, built a tunnel connecting his pool to ours. Soon, various guests of his backyard parties would swim through his tunnel and emerge in our pool, snorkels darting about aggressively, their goggles fogged. More and more unfamiliar men and women in aqua suits crawled up from the inner edges of our pool, congregating on the patio, saying they felt a yearning to strap scuba masks to their skulls and enter the mystery of the underwater tunnel.

Whenever we tried to confront Bill Poseidon about his tunneling into our pool, or initiate legal action against him, we felt a supernatural aquatic force, like a psychological water jet or tidal wave, pushing us back. One day while cleaning a desk, I happened upon the forgotten Dead Pool Scrolls from the bottom of the pool. Perhaps there was something in these stained cryptic words that could help us if we could only decipher the code.

The next day, I noticed the balding pool maintenance man. He was always trolling the neighborhood in his truck filled with insect nets, brushes, hoses, and chlorine supplies. I showed the Dead Pool Scrolls to him, and an ancient twinkle entered his eyes. "I can help you with this," he said slowly. "Meet me by your pool tonight at midnight."

At midnight, I met the balding pool maintenance man by the diving board of our pool. As usual, there were scuba-outfitted people from Bill Poseidon's tunnel, flopping around on our patio in their rubber fins. The balding pool maintenance man looked at the Dead Pool Scrolls and began chanting the words, as birds fluttered about. *"Oh whippoorwills in the whirlpool...it was meant to be a night of chlorination, but you congregated near water jet #1, leaving only water jet #2. Oh whippoorwills, end your shepherding of rubber-skinned invaders to our realm. Be gone, agents of Poseidon!"*

Upon completion of the chant, birds flew up out of the yard, and the aquatic force pulled the wetsuit-wearing scuba divers off of our patio, into the pool and Bill's tunnel. The tunnel hole then sealed itself and disappeared. I thanked the pool maintenance man. "All in a day's work," he said.

We never heard from Bill Poseidon again, but we still wanted to drain the water out of the pool. I was pleased over the next few months to see the cracks and vines return to the cement.

(originally published in **Winamop**)

Merle's Orchards

Merle walked through his orchards, the scent of nectarines and peaches filling his lungs. He kicked away tortoise shells as he ambled among rows of migrant workers. He settled next to the half-filled peach basket of Eduardo, who had just the other night crawled under the bullets and barbed wire into the "promised land". Eduardo was busily dumping peaches into the basket, brushing dust and bugs off his sleeves, when Merle said, "You know son, they just don't understand what it takes to run a place like this, I did all I could, but they just stare at me with their dark red eyes, you understand me, don't you?"

Eduardo looked at him and said, "The black crows are descending from the clouds to confiscate my soul, Merle. Fly into the dark weeds while you still have time!" Eduardo then slit his wrists with a razor blade he had saved from the morning's hygiene routine. He wavered and fell into the dirt at Merle's feet, his head resting in a pile of tortoise shells.

Merle staggered and set his eyes on Eduardo, thinking of the dark weeds and then pulling a Bible from his vest pocket, thumping it with a piece of flint. "You have laid yourself down for my sins, may the Lord dispatch you into the correct slot." And with that, he set about making arrangements for Eduardo's burial in a simple pine box in the orchards, as it seemed to be an easy method of body disposal.

Merle owned the county's general store near the orchards, and his tortoise Walter sat at Merle's feet on the store's front porch, dispensing information to the local population. Walter the Tortoise was a tortoise of integrity. A few years back, Jimmy Jones, the county's all-star high school quarterback, had impregnated a cheerleader and had sought Walter's advice. On the store porch, Walter puffed on a tiny corn-cob pipe that Merle had carved for him. "Now Jimmy, you must do the right thing and marry this girl," counseled Walter the Tortoise as Jimmy sat in rapt attention, nodding. "I trust that you won't disappoint me, young man," added Walter, engaging Jimmy in a paternal gaze.

On another occasion, the county had met on a proposal to extend the interstate through local farmland. Much of it would run through Farmer O'Hara's crops, toiled upon by generations of O'Hara's. "We mustn't let this happen!" spoke up an impassioned Walter the Tortoise at the county meeting. A megaphone was held up to Walter's little mouth as he spoke of how Farmer O'Hara had provided warmth and shelter in his barn for the birth of Maggie Johnston's bouncing baby boy, and how in the fall of '38, Grandpa O'Hara had shared his bumper marijuana crop at the town picnic, relieving the stress of the Great Depression and the gathering storm of fascism overseas. Farmer O'Hara had tears in his eyes as Walter exhorted, "We will protect every inch of land from these evil interlopers!" And they did. The freeway developers had offered local citizens an all-expenses-paid trip to Florida to see the 'Alligator of the Sun' up close, an experience guaranteed to bring personal transformation, in exchange for their support of the highway project. But they turned that down, thanks to Walter the Tortoise's oratory.

Merle reviewed Walter's accomplishments with pride, taking credit for them whenever possible. He assigned Walter more arduous tasks until one day Walter's shell shattered from overwork, his pieces strewn about on the general store's front porch. Merle was ready with a broom and dustpan, dispatching Walter's remains into the nearest appropriate wastebasket.

Years later, a wealthy Merle walked through his orchards with potential investors, post-dinner cigars and nectarine brandy on their breath. One of the investors blurted out, "You know Merle, your peaches and nectarines smell like death."

Merle pulled a peach from a tree, saying "Mighty good eating!" and chewed on it contentedly, displaying his gums to the investors, inviting them in for a bite, his wingtips grinding into soil and tortoiseshell chips. But this was the wrong peach to eat, as Merle slowly lost consciousness, blurry images of Eduardo and Walter passing through his mind, the black crows descending.

(originally published in *Clockwise Cat*)

Celeste

In the present life, Celeste and her boyfriend Edwin act upon their yearnings, encountering spilled seeds on car upholsteries during trysts on Lover's Lane. One night, they drive to a lake and swim in the dark water under the moonlight. On the shore they make love beneath the stars, promising their souls to each other forever. Soon Celeste becomes pregnant, and when she tells Edwin, he seems overjoyed, talking expansively of their future together. The next day, Edwin disappears, and Celeste drives around town looking for him, to no avail. As she drives by the lake where they had declared their undying love, she looks into her car's side view mirror, seeing a bright white light that pulls her back through time, into an earlier incarnation.

> In the past life, the river flowed with oil and black mud, salmon flipped onto the shore and died, coughing their salmon coughs, writhing on the sand. A car with a glowing side view mirror was parked nearby. "Looks like a grand day for boating," muttered Celeste, in an elegant dress and hat, holding a parasol with clenched fists. "Aye 'tis, Celeste!" declared Edwin, dressed as the gentleman dandy he was, in white pants, striped shirt, tie and straw hat. He was pulling mightily on the rope tied to a small boat, guiding it into the dock. They got in and started floating down the river, as a dark squid bounced out of the water and into the boat. Edwin swatted at it, worried that its squid movements would spray drops of mud on his immaculate white outfit. Celeste sat at the end of the boat, eyeing Edwin with suspicion, chewing on a piece of raw deer meat she had ripped off an abandoned carcass near the shore before boarding. Soon Edwin was on bended knee, asking for her hand in marriage. He held a ring out to Celeste, and she pinched it between her thumb and forefinger, examining it with a jeweler's magnifying glass from her purse. With an abrupt "Hmpph…" she threw the ring and the chewed deer carcass into the water, much to

the delight of the dark, muddy manta rays. Edwin jumped into the river after the ring and was sucked down into the mud. Celeste maneuvered the boat to the shore and walked toward the car, staring at the side door mirror's bright white light, which propelled her forward into the future.

In the future life, Celeste sits on the tan fabric of the cheap plastic chair. There is a faded rose pattern on the chair's cover, and the chair's frame squeaks disconcertingly as she shifts her weight. She drinks sweetened iced tea from a chipped glass adorned with prints of little owls. Her big black eyes are the first things that Edwin notices. He cannot find the whites of her eyes, only obsidian pools that seem to pull him in and smother, as he sits in the chair on the other side of the living room, nervously describing the insurance policy he is selling. Edwin's car is parked outside, the side view mirror shining. In the backyard, Celeste's two young children are playing with some broken misshapen toys on the brown crabgrass, a nearby sprinkler forlornly dripping water into the mud. In her faded yellow dress, Celeste never looks out the window at the children, only stares at Edwin with those big black unblinking eyes. Edwin continues his spiel, listing the benefits of the insurance policy, as the blackness of her eyes tears through him like a dagger and swims through his insides with a cancerous glow, finally pulling him down.

(originally published in *Yesteryear Fiction*)

Cosmic Sunflower Girl Fights Back

She is a relic from bygone hippie days, wandering the streets in colorful psychedelic dresses, a septuagenarian acid casualty. She'd had her time in the sunshine when she was known as Cosmic Sunflower Girl. Now, with her Day-Glo cane, she walks through strange corridors, trying to avoid the open manholes.

A cable news team, desperate for human interest stories, trolls the city in a van, looking for 'offbeat characters' representing the town's diverse human tapestry. The van pulls alongside as she is meandering along the sidewalk in a cloud of paisley mist. "Excuse me, ma'am, are you a hippie still living in the Summer of Love?" an interviewer in the van asks, smiling from behind a microphone.

"Banana vapor mist cartoon carrots sit around on the puffy woven chairs, a Frisbee in every mouth. Fetch! Fetch me a quid!" babbles Cosmic Sunflower Girl cryptically in response.

"This crazy old crone's exactly what we're looking for. Get her to spout some more of that drug-addled gibberish," whispers the producer to the interviewer.

"Wow that's trippy, lay some more on us grandma," smirks the interviewer, winking at the producer.

"I'm not in the mood to be a punch line for you patronizing, leeching parasites!" screams Cosmic Sunflower Girl suddenly at the interviewer in a moment of clarity, swinging her wooden Day-Glo cane wildly, splintering it to pieces as she shatters the van's windshield.

"Vicious old bat!" yells the interviewer in the van, as it lurches forward and speeds away.

A busybody nearby films the entire incident on his smartphone, offering some advice to Cosmic Sunflower Girl while pointing at what is left of her walking stick: "Perhaps you should have obtained a steel cane at whatever cane dispensary you patronized. If you had done so, you would not find yourself in the predicament you're now in," says the busybody as Cosmic Sunflower Girl limps around in traffic. She throws the remains of her cane at him and veers down the street unsteadily.

The incident is soon posted on the internet and goes viral. Cosmic Sunflower Girl becomes a celebrity hero to a group of bloggers who enthusiastically sing her praises: "SHE FIGHTS BACK AGAINST THE MEDIA!" "COSMIC SUNFLOWER GIRL BATTLES AGEISM!" "SHE SAYS 'NO' TO CALLOUS BUSYBODIES!" One of the bloggers buys her a new Day-Glo cane. A number of study groups are formed to examine and emulate her actions. When interviewed, Cosmic Sunflower Girl stares out from behind kaleidoscope eyeglasses and murmurs, "Red twinkling coronaries fly through the air, propelled by Bartokian green wings, sprinkling shreds of goodness to hungry citizens below, sticking tongues out to capture the stardust flavor emanating from the sky."

Soon there is talk of a Cosmic Sunflower Girl reality television show, and more people discuss what she will do next, what she thinks about various issues, what will be her next battle for individual rights and dignity. They search for nuggets of life-roadmap wisdom in her patchouli-soaked utterances.

Many people do not know that Cosmic Sunflower Girl rents an apartment inside a ramshackle yellow Victorian house. In the apartment, she is perched at an electronic command post that fills the living room. Surrounding her are assorted world maps, graphs, and beeps/blips of radar screens. Minions run about busily as Cosmic Sunflower Girl issues directives, on-task, razor-sharp: "Get me a read on Sector G, I want preliminary data on their marketing demographics," she orders, in the midst of developing what will become an empire of cosmic products. She thinks back to her past life as a fast-rising secretary at Acme Mega Corporation before she traded in her steno pad for love beads.

When asked about her plans as a celebrity, Cosmic Sunflower Girl's response is, "Dark green eucalyptus cream trees crawl up the vines of your mind. Bubbling moss flows through your soul in the blue aqua purifiers as you crawl into warm water inlets."

Additional study groups are formed to analyze Cosmic Sunflower Girl's statement, as her reality show goes into production.

(originally published in *Hobo Pancakes*)

Penguins

Horace sat in Antarctic research station 54, writing about penguins. He was in Antarctica on a government research grant, but the project was winding down, and he had time to wander and think, when not scribbling his research report with a frozen pen. He thought about how penguins had become a cute, cuddly animal for the cultural commerce subconscious. Horace decided to write a poem about motorized penguins, to illustrate what he saw as the corrupt commodification of the Antarctic flightless bird.

He sent the penguin poem to his sister Doris. Ever since being children, Horace and Doris had been very competitive with each other. Horace's poetic visions of the penguin conflicted with Doris' ideas of practicality. After reading the poem, Doris wrote a letter to Horace, telling him that penguin poetry would lead him nowhere.

As the weeks went by, Doris thought more about Horace's vision and decided to quickly develop a fleet of motorized penguins to be used in airports as a mode of baggage conveyance. Over the next few months, Doris would manage, via an instinctual eye during well-placed potluck dinners, to establish a network of connections that would enable her to lucratively install the motorized penguins in airports around the globe.

One day, as Doris worked on her bird fleet, she noticed a tag on one of the penguins, which said, 'Inspected by Number 54'. "I just tore this tag off the other day," she said to herself. "I know I did." She began to experience that uneasy feeling again, so she walked across the hall into her husband Gus' den.

Weatherman Gus paced about the den. "Where's my motorized penguin?" he blurted, "I need to know!"

"Stop babbling dear," said Doris. "Look at this tag, what does it mean?"

"It means Inspected by Number 54," said Weatherman Gus with a wry grin. "HEH-HEH-HA-HA-HA!!!!"

"God, help him," thought Doris. Whatever happened to that

strapping young 'Weather Guy' she had married? He had been the darling of the Channel 54 news, wearing his toupees with flair, and turning the ancient television weatherman task of writing temperature numbers on glass backward into an art. A motorized penguin whizzed by in the hallway and Doris let out a sigh of relief. "Well thank goodness, at least there's something I can rely on," she said, busying herself with her ever-growing army of motorized birds.

In a letter from Antarctica, Horace asked Doris for some money, as it had been his poem that inspired her business success with the motorized penguins. In response, Doris had Gus send a weather bulletin to Horace at the research station, predicting 'cold'.

Undaunted, Horace thought more about penguins. "I have recurrent dreams of a nurturing penguin, leading me down important avenues of this incarnation. I need to provide protective fabrics for these guiding lights," he said, writing a poem about penguin sweaters and sending it to Doris.

Upon reading Horace's poem, Doris checked with her potluck dinner connections, who confirmed that "penguins will become the 'Pet du jour', as pigs were previously, among the cultural elite in New York & Los Angeles. As low-temperature pet habitats are created in various dwellings, penguin sweaters will be in high demand. A penguin will be nude without one!"

"The temperature is 54 degrees Fahrenheit," reported Weatherman Gus.

Doris started a lucrative penguin sweater business, based on Horace's poem. She offered him no royalties, but this time Horace hired a good lawyer, and successfully sued her in court.

Carpet

"What's that filthy-looking liquid you're pouring on the carpet?" demanded Belle during the cocktail party.

"It's what's left of my soul," Ron replied, eyeing the fluid, and the watery ice cubes that fell on the avocado-colored shag carpeting.

"Oh, don't be so dramatic," said Belle, lifting her finger to signal white-suited minions, who hurried in and began an extensive scrubbing operation, using brightly-colored sponges to remove the stain.

"The pink in the liquid is a residue of my brain, and the runny red is the blood, sweat and tears you have wrung out of me in our relationship," Ron added as Belle supervised the scrubbing operation.

"Do you ever look at this from my perspective? Do you know how much work I do to keep things on track?" she queried as one of the minions moved from the carpet, and began scrubbing the toes of her white plastic boots.

Prone on the carpet, Ron drifted into a dream, encountering his identity from a past life:

> *"I'm Roy, I run the neighborhood hardware store on Saturday mornings and beyond. I have sharp, penetrating eyes, but a friendly manner. I have been here forever and will remain here throughout eternity. I chain-smoke and fantasize about committing bizarre sexual crimes. 'Yes, a radio transistor, sir? Right away.' I live in a faded yellow house in a respectable tree-lined neighborhood. I fix the neighborhood's bicycles and kites, with a bright sparkle in my eye. Why are you judging me?"*

In the past life, Belle's earlier soul had been Roy's 9th victim.

Ron licked Belle's white boots and she kicked him in the teeth. He slathered around on the heavy fabric, looking for molar remnants, and she kicked him some more, spilling blood onto the carpet.

(originally published in *In Between Altered States*)

Hairdryers of Obedience

"I can look up at the stars and moon, feel the wind on my face. They can't take that away from me," said Zelda on her way to a political group meeting, wracked with worry about her precarious position in the group's hierarchy. On her way to the discussion gathering, Zelda realized her supply of wrenches was low and ducked into a hardware store along the way. Behind the screws, wrenches, hammers, pipes and sprinklers, were 4 people sitting on orange plastic chairs under industrial strength hairdryers, reading old 'Field & Stream' and 'Cosmopolitan' magazines.

One of the persons said, "Helen Gurley Brown has often, in the most difficult of circumstances, been beneficent," but would not elaborate beyond this cryptic oration. The hairdryers were all connected by a tangled web of cords and cables to a small glass box in the lawnmower section of the hardware store. Inside the box was a brain suspended in green liquid. The hairdryers were colored bright blue, red, yellow and purple, one word on each, combining to spell out, 'The Hairdryers of Obedience.'

Zelda stared at the front of the Cosmopolitan magazine being read under Hairdryer #2, fixating upon the workman-like pupils of the cover model. The magazine sizzled and erupted into flame, the smoke forming the figure of one Nanette X, wearing a wildly colored floral smock and sitting down under a mammoth 1956 faded beige and pink hairdryer in the corner of the room, reading a copy of 'Agricultural Cavalcade'. Nanette cackled gleefully, dentures falling out of her mouth onto the floor, snapping up and down, moving menacingly along the linoleum towards Zelda, beckoning her to sit down under the next hairdryer. Zelda hesitated, but then maneuvered into the orange plastic chair next to Nanette, who bellowed, "Now honey, I'm going to invade your psyche and stomp around in there in my open-toed pumps!"

Zelda felt a strange onrushing acquiescence as some important words trampled into her head from the hairdryer, though she couldn't quite make out what they were. The hairdryer then switched off, and Nanette X, now all business, instructed Zelda to proceed to the hardware store cashier. After paying for her wrenches, Zelda left the hardware store and walked to the political meeting.

The group leader flew through the front door, agenda in hand. "Today we will form a committee to review the actions of last week's committee, and we will have a referendum on Zelda's vice-chairmanship of this organization," she announced quickly, distributing the agenda to those in the room, all seated on creaky metal chairs.

"The ping-pong balls are in the tar," reminded Ronald, who had been promoted to lieutenant. "They look like eggs deposited in the La Brea tar pits!"

"Thank you, Ronald, but try to stay on task!" admonished the group leader, chalk grinding into the blackboard at the front of the room. Zelda listened to the left-wing propaganda that was filling her ears after the right-wing propaganda had filled her ears last week. She closed her eyes and envisioned Nanette X in her turbulently hued floral smock, laughing madly under the hairdryer, dentures snapping about.

"I have a motion I'd like to make," announced Ronald, standing up importantly. The group leader glared at him. Zelda turned toward the group leader, and walked out of the room, out the building, and onto the sidewalk, her own agenda ahead.

(originally published in *Seahorse Rodeo Folk Review*)

The Weathermen

Rain or shine, the weathermen emerged in white tribal raincoats, ready for prognostications of meteorological disturbances, eyeing their weather charts and radar systems. They congregated at the coastal lighthouse and ran inside to scribble predictions on ancient parchments. Later, more weathermen entered the lighthouse, assembling for coffee and cheesecake, clicking the lighthouse signal light on and off in their milling and gathering.

The ship that floated in the sea, adjacent to the jagged rocks, was confused by the signals from the lighthouse, moving port and starboard, then into the black. The boat ripped its hull against the jagged stone, crashing into the doomed port of the rock island in the night. The seamen crawled out of the wrecked vessel onto the cold grey rocks, gasping for air. They climbed through the icy night to the lighthouse, only to find its door closed, no weathermen to be found.

Eventually, the seamen were discovered by extreme picnickers, who enjoyed perching their picnic baskets on broken shards of shale. The picnickers shuttled the seamen back to civilization, where they were bathed, clothed and reassigned to a new boat. The weathermen chartered this boat to observe weather phenomena out at sea. The seamen got their revenge on the weathermen by abandoning them on a small rock in the middle of the ocean. There the weathermen sat in their white tribal raincoats, scribbling notes busily on clipboards. Eventually, the weathermen were rescued by the extreme picnickers, who were scuba diving with aqua-compatible picnic baskets.

(originally published in *Postcard Shorts*)

Shadow Traffic

"Fran, I need you to go to the gas station and fill up the minivan, can you manage to do that without screwing it up?" her husband asked derisively.

"Yes of course," said Fran, numbed by now to his constant criticism. As he stalked out the door to work, he just looked like a puppet fading into the fog.

Fran pulled into her favorite nearby service station and was greeted by the attendant. "Fill it up, please, Dave," said Fran, staring dreamily as unleaded gas was pumped into the minivan.

Through a cloud, Fran saw the shadow woman pull a car into the service station on a desolate desert highway, noticing the sign, which read 'All Services Permitted'. The shadow woman pulled up to the first pump, labeled 'Evil', pumped evil into the car's gas tank, and then gave the cashier her credit card. The cashier's eyes gleamed brightly as he ran the credit card through the machine. The shadow woman's credit card activity statement would later just show the word 'Evil' in the credit column for that transaction, which would end up requiring a number of phone calls to the bank to get things straightened out. As the shadow woman left the service station, the cashier happily plunked the black key on the cash register with his index finger, the sign 'Another Sale' ringing up.

Fran drove to the community center and cheerfully added her input to the town discussion on traffic solutions. "I think there should be a few more 'Stop' and 'Yield' signs set up to protect our citizens," she suggested.

Staring into the grey nylon carpeting of the community center, Fran saw the shadow woman think about the city traffic patterns and respond, "Well I think that the legs should be cut off the bodies in the morgue, and little wheels attached to the bottoms of their feet." The shadow woman continued, "A television set could be attached to the top of the legs in the space previously occupied by the torso. The entire contraption should then be spray painted sky-blue. After that, road maintenance would get involved. Every road should have an electric trolley groove embedded in it. Then we place the wheels of the sky-blue tv-legs into the groove and have them slide up and down the streets day and night. The televisions would provide information and entertainment to traffic and pedestrians, and the legs would provide a humanistic touch. Also, this device could be painted a different color if the sky-blue doesn't blend in well with the particular locale."

As Fran saw the dark apparition slowly disappear into the community center carpeting, she received approval for her suggestion of more 'Stop' and 'Yield' signs. She got back into the minivan and drove home.

"Well, did you accomplish the tasks I assigned to you?" demanded her husband at dinner.

"Yes dear," said Fran, staring at her husband's torso while slicing roast beef and imagining new traffic solutions. Tomorrow she would have to clear up some odd entries on her credit card and figure out why there were blue mannequin legs in the back of the minivan.

(originally published in *Weirdyear*)

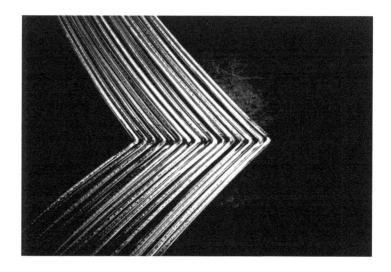

Couples and Bees

Roy and Mavis were on the golf course committing atrocities, slamming golf clubs into the heads of unsuspecting rodents found in the underbrush. "We have ancient historical precedence and imperative!" declared Mavis, leaning back in the seat of the golf cart, chewing crackers, a big black tattered book propped up on the scorecard clamp. "From Chapter 79385, 'Roam freely, conquer the earth, and strike down the rats and hornets!'"

"I like the cut of your jib, and the angle of your gait, Mavis," said Roy, bringing a 3-iron down on the head of a snowy egret, approving of her twisted interpretation. After an hour, Roy and Mavis maneuvered their golf cart off the course and onto the sidewalks of the nearby suburban neighborhood, thinking of their in-laws Bill & Harriet and Edna & Edward frequently, looking for pets to subdue. A bee took notice of their activities.

The mist was rising over the tundra as Bill and Harriet flipped through the TV listings. They thought of their in-laws Roy and Mavis infrequently while sitting on matching Barcaloungers in the frozen wasteland, chain-smoking cigarettes. "Where is my cummerbund?" muttered Bill intensely.

Suddenly bees flew up out of the ground, and lined up, staring at Bill and Harriet confrontationally, hands on hips, or legs on thorax. "We demand to know why you are invading and soiling our landscape with your man-made garbage!" yelled one of the bees, Beatrice, who had appointed herself spokesbee (spokesperson), despite contrary opinion among the group.

"I'm late for the dance, I've just been trying to get to the dance all this life, that's all I've been trying to do. Right now I'm looking for my cummerbund!" Bill said defensively.

"We will lead you to it," said the bees as they gathered together in a buzzing roar around Bill and Harriet.

"No, no please don't sting us to death!" yelled the two Homo sapiens.

The bees said quietly, "No, we wouldn't do that," and instead each of the bees gave Bill and Harriet a light, gentle kiss, sending them into dreamy ecstasy.

"Edna, don your tennis smock now! We must frolic, but it will be frolicking with a purpose!" cried Edward jauntily.

Edna looked up from her knitting, with a raised eyebrow. "Have you gone off your meds, Edward? The chicken croquettes and fruit salad must be prepared by midnight! What kind of cook are you?"

Edward had been charged with preparing hors d'ouevres at the Von Goffstead estate. "Again Edna, I am not a cook, I am a food technician!"

Edna eyed her knitting needle which started to resemble a bee stinger, and yelled, "But a technician gone haywire!"

"Edna, with a playful jab!" retorted Edward. He returned to the kitchen, announcing as soup exploded from the stove pot, flying onto the wall, "The seasonings are having a lively battle over which one will dominate the taste of the soup!" A few weeks earlier, during what Edward called 'a vigorous session of sautéing', a kitchen fire burnt the east wing of the house to the ground. He looked at the clock, "Edna, we must play tennis soon, it is urgent!"

Edna had dreamt of her free soul streaming through the trees, earth, water and air. She turned to Edward as bees flew through a vent, flooding the room, "I'm sorry, Edward, but I cannot be held in by the boundary lines of the tennis court!" Edna threw down her knitting, clutched a tennis racquet with a quickly-evolving beehive at the end, and marched into the nearby forest.

Edward returned to his work in the kitchen, pouring gasoline into a frying pan, then retreated into Van Goffstead's study, reading Chaucer, babbling about the end of the world.

Roy swerved the golf cart to avoid a swarm of bees. He and Mavis tumbled out and bumped their heads on the sidewalk. Rising dizzied, they ran to the nearby hardware center to begin a career selling lawn care appliances and jars of fruit-flavored honey door-to-door on the A.M. shift, happily enduring the wrath of awakened neighbors, and cultists clad in white shirts and black ties, thumping tomes and complaining with clenched fists that it was 'their turf' as sweat poured from their brows in the morning heat. Roy and Mavis became insistent about lawn clippers, and no longer clubbed wildlife with 3-woods. Wherever they went, a few bees followed.

(originally published in *The Mustache Factor*)

Weekend

Wild porcupines chewed on my right eyeball, and then scurried purposefully across the green kitchen tile, hoping for an opportune spot under the large grey chandelier, helpfully installed by the Chandelier Support Team, a fellowship of like-minded ceiling-light enthusiasts. Below the chandelier we occupied the hardwood floor, sucking on varnished wood grain, dozing, or otherwise horizontal for reasons known only to us. We don't know why the strange bird flew through the window, pecked busily at our eyes, and brought its odd ways with eggs of mystery into our apartment. We found a blue egg near the ashtray in the living room, a red egg located near the clothes hamper in the hall closet, and a green egg suspended near the garbage disposal. I decided that I had to leave the eggs alone and proceed out of the apartment until the eggs could be exterminated by a professional removal team wearing white space suits, wielding flamethrowers and large industrial vacuums with impressive capabilities. Leaving the apartment, I chose to follow the moss in the hallway, leading outside. I crawled along the moss towards the beach, where I could be more in touch with the eels, jellyfish, and strange one-celled creatures of our ancestry. When I reached the water, I boarded a faded green rowboat, grabbed both its oars, and rowed out into the water. In the middle of the bay, I had an epiphany that I should try to use my left hand more in general activities (I'm right-handed), to get more of a feeling of newness, discovery, refreshment, hope, and aliveness. I dropped the right oar, clutched the left oar, and rowed in circles for hours, not proceeding forward. I'm not sure what kind of lesson this taught me, or if it was a lesson at all. Instead of using the right oar to get back to shore I decided to activate the small outboard motor that had been helpfully placed in a small compartment of the boat by an unknown entity. I reflected on the implications that this reliance on technology had, and I decided that I envied the lizard that had crawled up from the bottom of the boat and was chewing on my left eyeball. Soon I was back in my air-conditioned, yet heated apartment, cooking omelets consisting of the colored eggs that still remained, and weaving aerated pillows with a passion that I had never felt before. I wasn't sure whether my new-found passion for weaving aerated pillows would lead to an internet-based business, beholden to the tenets of cyber commerce, but I was willing to cast my lot with this wave of economic promise. At my computer, I decided to play Angry Birds instead. I got through a number of levels, but was frustrated by Level 4, as it had too many slabs of wood and ice. I decided to examine the motivations of the Angry Birds and saw purple voluptuous caterpillars lounge about on straw mats demanding more nourishment. "We're living the extreme lifestyle!" declared one of the caterpillars, a straw in its little mouth, ingesting industrial nectar. "Why not?" asked another, multitasking, feeding spoons of sugar and sand to the illiterate walking wounded. The birds of longing fluttered down to the straw mats and admired the ethos of the purple voluptuous caterpillars. "Upon what intellectual theory have you based your way of living?" asked one of the birds, an egret wearing a tasteful suede overcoat. "We follow the ways of the impala," said the caterpillars quickly, looking up at a clay impala replica at the top of the hill, sunlight shining flatly off of its kiln-baked surface. "What are the ways of the impala?" asked one of the birds, a parrot, way too quickly. The caterpillars looked at the bird suspiciously and went silent. The other birds stared at the parrot with disdain. "We have been longing for this knowledge and you had to compromise our position. Do you know how many weeks of planning and preparation went into this operation?" As the parrot's eyes were pecked out by the Angry Birds, I entered the kitchen, seeing purple voluptuous caterpillars crawling over the 'Puree' button on the blender, and I decided that I wanted to make dinner for a number of neighbors and cats in the apartment complex. The cats were more interested in my culinary efforts, and I decided that I would reward them with a basket full of slippers made out of mice (the toes of the slippers being especially tasty). I then slept a few more hours, and now I'm back to work on Monday, doing whatever it is that I do.

(originally published in *The Mustache Factor*)

A Late Dinner

An industrious whirr was heard from the kitchen as dessert was prepared. Everybody had enjoyed the stuffed pheasant, feathers drifting out of our mouths as we awaited the orange marmalade tart. We all ordered coffee, except for Ted, who demanded a berry-flavored Hi-C fruit drink in a yellow plastic mug reminiscent of his childhood. "Yes sir!" said the waiter.

We were at an economic policy conference, and a number of informative presentations had been made throughout the day. My colleague on the economic panel, Ted, gave a particularly impressive speech on the implications of tax policy on global financial trade. But now the presentations were over, and we were well into dinner, late in the evening.

Ted voiced his discomfort with his chair, it was too low. He wanted something higher, much higher. The waiters looked around in the back and returned with a baby's high chair. Ted eyed the chair favorably as the waiters lifted him up onto the seat, Ted's black wingtips gouging one of them in the neck. Ted was settled into the chair, a little security strap fastened across his chest, overlapping his suit, shirt, vest and tie, his black shoes and socks dangling above the floor. Dessert was served. Ted stuffed some of the orange marmalade tart into his mouth, and the waiter quickly wiped the pastry goo from his face with a napkin.

Ted's pant legs swung wildly in the high chair as he emphasized the economic merits of free trade during a serious discussion with the Minister of Finance from the Far East. Ted pulled the little yellow plastic mug of Hi-C to his lips for another delicious sip. "Ted, are you attempting to channel your inner child? Perhaps you're participating in a session of hypnotic regression to childhood," said one of his dinner companions, a weathered dowager in a blue dress. Ted promptly bopped her on the head with a purple rattle that was set on the plastic tray of the high chair by one of the waiters.

After finishing his orange marmalade tart, and throwing pieces of it at the other guests, Ted noticed the black 'X' imprinted on his cup saucer. "What does this 'X' mean, Ted?" asked the weathered dowager, holding the cup saucer in front of his eyeballs, assaulting his pupils. Ted had been seeing the black 'X' for the last few weeks on billboards, economic reports, and up in the sky. He climbed down from the high chair and looked out the window. There was a beautiful beach outside. Ted excused himself discreetly and walked outside, down to the beach. Nearby was an old amusement park, where Ted had played when he was a child. He set his feet on the sand and walked along the waves the rest of the night.

The next day, Ted sat in a little 6.5-foot plastic pool in his front yard, wearing a gray suit and tie, playing with boats and inflatable animals, belying his 20-year reputation as a stable, reasonable voice in the world economic discussion. The Minister of Finance from the Far West was at the side of the inflatable pool, holding important documents for Ted to sign. As Ted moved toward the contracts, he saw the little plastic duck with the black 'X' on its side bobbing along with cheer and purpose.

Ted knew the black 'X' was cancer that had been moving quickly through his body. When he had learned of it weeks ago, he started reviewing his life, trying to relive early joys, as his time ran down. When the plastic duck reached him, Ted knew his life was at an end, and he succumbed, sinking to the bottom of the plastic inflatable pool, but it was nice to be back in his childhood one more time.

(originally published in *Weirdyear*)

Sudoku

By the remote lake in the meadow on the mountain, Mrs. Snaff sat working on the Sudoku puzzle, acolytes at her feet, working on their own Sudoku puzzles, looking up at her questioningly. "What are the answers? What are the clues?" they asked in quiet unison, gazing up at Mrs. Snaff in her long dark robe, her No. 2 pencil scribbling furiously.

"There is no answer," she answered cryptically to the baffled students. "Understand the goal," she patiently told the pupils. "You must complete the 9x9 grid so that every row, column and 3x3 box contains every digit from 1 to 9 inclusively. The path to enlightenment lies in the process, not the result."

An earnest young student looked up at Mrs. Snaff, eyes full of wonder, "What does it say about the process when my pencil has snapped?" A roar of thunder was heard as a cold rain started to fall in the lush green mountain meadow.

Mrs. Snaff's keen eyes spied the minuscule shard of cracked lead on the ground near the student's left foot. "Sometimes the path is arduous," she replied mysteriously, returning to her puzzle as the pupils contemplated this concept, and the wind blew through the meadow.

(originally published in *Postcard Shorts*)

Sprinklers

'Do what you love' was the message of a self-help book that Sam was reading on his lunch break at Acme Mega Corporation. He worked in the sewage billing division, processing invoices for plumbing fixtures and toilet components. Sam was not doing what he loved.

Looking up from the book, Sam gazed out the window at the manicured lawn of the corporate office park. His eyes were drawn to the lawn sprinkler jets about 20 feet away. One sprinkler jet was situated in such a way that its angle in relation to the oleander and juniper plants nearby triggered in his brain chemistry a vision of a group of men riding bicycles on the edge of a cliff, each of them wearing a long, white lab coat with a big black question mark on the back. Exactly one-half of the men have their vision filtered through a symmetric set of purple dots. The other men have their vision filtered through the nozzle of a lawn sprinkler, water pouring down into their faces, covered in moss and weeds. "I want to be one of those men," Sam told himself intensely. "I want to be around lawn sprinklers!"

Sam quit his job at Acme Mega Corporation, started to read up on yard care, and practiced sprinkler valve repair. He became romantically involved with a gardening department assistant named Sonia from the local home improvement store. Late at night, after the home improvement store had closed, Sonia would use her key to open the door to the gardening department, where she and Sam would make love atop sacks of fertilizer, sprawling amidst plant seeds and garden hoses, Sonia's screams of ecstasy causing the rhododendron leaves to vibrate with embarrassment.

Sam gradually built up a reputation for lawn maintenance, and the neighbors started to seek his help. Sam enjoyed his work immensely, and soon developed a thriving lawn irrigation business. Sam's relationship with Sonia was also blooming, and they decided to get married. The wedding ceremony took place at a botanical garden, where the sprinklers shot water up into the sky after Sam and Sonia said their vows.

One Saturday, Sam was recalibrating the sprinkler system of his next-door neighbors Don and Judy Henshaw, who were in a fierce argument over their lawn care. Judy preferred their current Rain-Bird sprinklers, whereas Don opted for drip irrigation. Sam had been brought in to do some repairs, and analyze the situation.

It started to rain, which Sam liked to think of as "nature's sprinkler system". The Henshaws asked Sam if he'd like to stop, as he was getting soaked by the water pouring out of the sky. "No, thank you!" called Sam cheerily. He loved his work, and he loved Sonia. After life had been so difficult in the past, things couldn't be better! He smiled up at the sky as he walked towards another lawn jet. That's when he slipped on the wet grass and fell, impaling himself on a sharp sprinkler head. Spilling out blood, Sam's prone body triggered the repaired sprinkler system, which sprayed water on his splayed carcass, every 12 seconds. Through a blurring eye, Sam saw images of Sonia, while the sprinklers sprayed water reliably. As his blood soaked into the lawn, providing nutrients, Sam went out doing what he loved.

(originally published in *Mad Swirl*)